Produc

Highly Effective Strategies to Develop Grit,
Discipline, Stop Addictions

(Goal Setting Guide to Measure Only What
Really Matters by Using Data Science the Agile
Way)

Chris K. Glei

Published by Kevin Dennis

© **Chris K. Glei**

All Rights Reserved

Productivity: Highly Effective Strategies to Develop Grit, Discipline, Stop Addictions (Goal Setting Guide to Measure Only What Really Matters by Using Data Science the Agile Way)

ISBN 978-1-989920-96-1

Legal & Disclaimer

The information contained in this book is not designed to replace or take the place of any form of medicine or professional medical advice. The information in this book has been provided for educational and entertainment purposes only.

The information contained in this book has been compiled from sources deemed reliable, and it is accurate to the best of the Author's knowledge; however, the Author cannot guarantee its accuracy and validity and cannot be held liable for any errors or omissions. Changes are periodically made to this book. You must consult your doctor or get professional medical advice before using any of the suggested remedies, techniques, or information in this book.

Upon using the information contained in this book, you agree to hold harmless the Author from and against any damages, costs, and expenses, including any legal fees potentially resulting from the application of any of the information provided by this guide. This disclaimer applies to any damages or injury caused by the use and application, whether directly or indirectly, of any advice or information presented, whether for breach of contract, tort, negligence, personal injury, criminal intent, or under any other cause of action.

You agree to accept all risks of using the information presented inside this book. You need to consult a professional medical practitioner in order to ensure you are both able and healthy enough to participate in this program.

Table of Contents

Introduction

Have you ever told yourself these words? You, my friend, have experienced procrastination. While we only have 24 hours in a day, sometimes it's just not possible to complete the things we set out to do. Often times, it's because we haven't been taught how to. When we don't accomplish the things we want or even need to, we are hugely damaging not only our health mentally and physically, but our ability to achieve the bigger dreams we have in our lives.

Procrastination, perfectionism, and generally putting things off can lead to increased anxiety and feelings of depression. More importantly, it can and will detract from actually achieving anything you want to accomplish. If you want to live happier and more stress-free it is important to be able to recognize the signs of procrastination, why you do it, and figure out how to overcome it. You will learn how to set deadlines that really motivate you to get work done. You will read how to make a schedule and stick to it. You will learn the importance of tactile engagement and write down goals. You will be exposed to what to do with your incomplete tasks and where to work in order to overcome procrastination. You will design your daily routine and what things you can do to maximize it. You will learn how to work with your body's clock and not against it, utilizing the best times for productivity. By monitoring your time and using peak times wisely you will learn that your body is a tool for beating procrastination. We will also cover the importance of taking breaks and exercising regularly in a method of overcoming procrastination that is not just about efficiency but about your health.

More importantly, you will be taught how you can remain realistic and practical in the goals you are setting. Part of this achievement means avoiding perfectionism. Good health, foods and hydration, and cognitive exercises can improve the way your brain works for the better, increasing your productivity. Finally, you will learn the importance of a good reward system regarding keeping yourself motivated.

So if you are ready to get over your procrastination, it's time to take action and really get it done not another day, but right now.

Chapter 1: Location, Location, Location

Most people do not put much thought into where it is that they will be performing their tasks. Of course, some chores will not offer you the luxury of mobility. If what you need to do is fix the car, you will have to go to the garage. If the window in the bedroom needs repairing, you have no choice but to go to the bedroom. There are many times, however, when your tasks will be more mobile. Take, for instance, studying for a test. Or reading a book for class. Or finishing a sales presentation for work. These things are able to be completed in a variety of places and choosing the correct one for you may be more important than you think.

To begin, let's discuss the basics of brain-training. You may not be aware of it but your brain is able to subconsciously perceive patterns. Your mind understands things even if you are not fully aware of its understanding. Specifically, your brain can be trained to correlate a particular location to a particular task. In other words, your mind can prepare you to better perform a duty if that duty is always performed in the same place.

How, exactly, does this relate to being more productive? If, for instance, you always study at the desk in the bedroom, you are more likely to be productive by continuing to study at that location. Do not underestimate your brain's ability to associate an area with one thing and only one thing. For example, if you study in many different places at many different times, there is no consistency to your productivity. If you walk past the dining room, you likely have no particular mental association with that room. It's the room you eat in, the room you talk in, the room you walk through. Many things happen in that room. If, however, you make a concerted effort to always study in the same place, that place then becomes the designated study place in your mind. If you make that place the basement, for instance, you now know that when it's time to study, it's time to go to the basement. You get down there and the stability of always performing the same activity at the same spot registers, and your brain is actually more focused on the task at hand.

Furthermore, you can setup this location with all the practical tools you will need to continue being productive. Make it a very serious workstation. By doing this you will allow yourself to stay in that location until the task is finished. Many times it's easy to begin losing focus simply by leaving the area in an attempt to collect the proper materials. Be organized and make sure that your workstation has everything you need. There is no need to stray. Once you are there, it is the right time to jump on those tasks.

Chapter 2: Dealing With Negativity

Your positive action combined with positive thinking results in success." – Shiv Khera

Negativity stops you in your tracks. If you find that your life is surrounded by it, you will never be truly happy until you can do something about it. When you feel negative, there is cloud over your life that you can lift very easily if you want to. If you are unhappy, chances are that much of that unhappiness is caused by your approach to life, rather than by other people. Take responsibility for it and let go of it by following the habits in this chapter.

Habit No. 2 – Stop talking negatively to yourself

When you do this, you reinforce negativity and that makes the negativity grow. You are giving credence to thoughts that bring you down. I would suggest that you choose a happy song that you like and every time that you find yourself talking negatively to yourself, you actively replace this with your happy song, even if only sung in your head. You need to get rid of negative thinking. It will not allow you to be happy and you will be forever berating yourself for your shortcomings. Everyone has shortcomings. Accept them for what they are and they don't become unmanageable.

Habit No. 3 – Get rid of Negative influences

You may not realize it but people around you can bring you down and make you negative. You need to write down the names of all the people that you know and work out which ones are toxic to your wellbeing. These will be people who use you, who are constantly criticizing you and who make demands of you without giving anything back. You have to learn to say "no" to this kind of person, because all the time you devote to doing tasks for them, you are depriving yourself of time to be doing things you actually enjoy.

Habit No. 4 – Gratitude

When you see through the eyes of someone who is always unhappy, you find ingratitude. In every single day of your life, there is something to be grateful for. Start keeping a journal and write down the things that you are grateful for every morning before you get out of bed. If you start the day in this way, what you are doing is reinforcing positive thinking. If you struggle to find something, here are a few suggestions:

You have a roof over your head.

You have good weather.

You have your health.

You have the use of all of your limbs.

You are not deaf or blind.

Habit No. 5 – Acknowledge your strengths

We are so busy telling ourselves off for the things that we fail to do that sometimes, we don't see the things that we are good at. Loving yourself opens you up to love and there's nothing wrong with congratulating yourself on small successes well done. For example, you may not see it as important, but the first time that you manage to clean all of your house, enjoy it. Get rid of things in your life that get in the way of happiness because when you declutter your life, you make life so much easier to handle. In other words, be happy with your small victories. Be generous of spirit and enjoy who you are because this is the first step toward true happiness.

The one thing about negativity is that it only lasts as long as you acknowledge it and allow it to take a hold in your life. The moment you let go of negativity, life gets better and you are able to achieve much more. Don't let others bring you down either. If you need to free yourself from negative people, then do so. Don't stop to feel bad about it because you are doing yourself the biggest favor possible and perhaps in the process are teaching people around you to stop being negative. Usually people who are miserable enjoy the effect they have on others in making them miserable too. Don't let that become who you are. They can always take their negativity out on someone else.

Chapter 3: The Real Reason You Keep Procrastinating

Novelist Ellen Glasgow said that the strongest motive, whether we are conscious of it or not, rules our conduct. This chapter can make us conscious of our motives and underlying reasons for procrastination. The insights can help us develop strategies to stop procrastinating and start being proactive.

Choices, Choices, Choices

When talking about procrastination, it's always a choice between alternatives.

Choosing pleasure over pain, pleasant over unpleasant

Remember that time when you chose to watch television instead of doing your homework? Or when you just tinkered with your mobile phone all day instead of doing household chores?

Procrastination is a coping mechanism to anticipated stress, anxiety, and fatigue. From an evolutionary perspective, this is related to the flight response that made our ancestors choose the less painful path. Instead of fighting a raging tiger, they would just run away and hide.

But in our modern world, where there are no immediate threats of being eaten by wild animals, the "flight response" to perceived objects or situations of stress only prolongs our agony. Tigers may go away, but assignments and dishes won't do themselves.

Choosing easy over difficult, simple over overwhelming

Remember that time when you chose to shred scratch papers instead of starting to write your report due the next day? Less urgent and menial tasks appear less daunting, so you choose to carry them out instead of more urgent and important matters. It is convenient to choose urgent tasks that are easy to execute over important goals or tasks that need planning.

Sometimes, it can also be because you have too much on your plate already that you don't know where to start. Or maybe your workload or list of to-do's is not organized. Feeling overwhelmed, you just do the simplest task on your list, just to tick something off.

Remember also when you do band-aid solutions but failed to follow through? For instance, when you invited your friends over, but felt too lazy to clean up, so you just threw a blanket over your cluttered chairs, then kept it there for months? It is tempting to resort to quick fixes.

While you are busy doing menial tasks and resorting to quick fixes, the clock is ticking. That report won't write itself and the chairs won't declutter on their own.

Choosing to see a task as an imposition over opportunity

This is deeper and less primal than pleasure versus pain and easy versus difficult choices. This is when we perceive a task to be an unwelcome demand that requires too much from us, or requires resources that we lack, such as time and skills.

Maybe you had this thought before, when someone asked you to do something: "I don't have time to do what you want me to do."

Or perhaps: "I don't know how to do it, I still need to figure out how to do it, so I will take my time. In the meantime, let me digress..."

The way to deal with this is to separate emotions, assumptions, and personal issues from the task at hand. Consider the task for what it is, as something that needs to be done. What do you need in order to do it? That is your opportunity to grow and thrive.

Choosing perfection over progress

This is common among perfectionists. They either do it perfectly, or they do not do it at all. They either nail it or evade it.

Maybe you have been putting off doing interior design on your apartment until you finish disposing of your clutter, which you find too tedious to start doing. You say you don't have time. Years passed, you still have your clutter and your apartment still needs redesigning. Maybe you should make time already?

Or maybe you have been delaying finishing a long-overdue report because inspiration to have a perfect finished product is elusive. Months passed, and your boss issues you a memo that you took as an imposition. You finished the report anyway, and it surprised you that it took you only 2 hours to finish a good output. It took you months to finish it in 2 hours.

Indeed, whether you are a perfectionist or not, when you finally get things done, you feel like a thorn has been pulled off, you feel weight coming off your shoulders, and a general sense of accomplishment. Hold on to this positive feeling, and keep it in mind the next time you think about procrastinating.

Choosing to escape in the moment over moving forward

Living in the moment is a mindful thing to do, but not when it becomes your delaying tactic or escape.

Maybe as a teen, you would sneak out to party instead of studying for an exam. Or as an adult, you would drink rather than face a problem. Some people turn to vices as a scapegoat to actual problems.

After partying and drinking, when you're sober, the issues and problems remain.

"Impulse, immediate, short-term" over "deliberate, enduring, long-term"

Do you delay tasks and enjoy immediate albeit short-lived gratification? Or do you do tasks immediately and enjoy delayed albeit fulfilling sense of gratification?

Bottom line, it's a choice between impulse and deliberate, immediate or enduring, short-term or long-term.

Factors that Influence the Choice to Procrastinate

It is also vital to understand what goes behind the choice to delay. Here are just some factors that can make us procrastinate. The power to reverse procrastination lies within these influences as well.

Brain regions

At the heart of all these choices is the interaction between our limbic system and prefrontal cortex. Limbic system is our inner child that seeks immediate gratification and thrives on emotions and impulse decisions. Meanwhile, the prefrontal cortex is the region for planning and decision-making, serving as our inner adult. For Freudians, it is the id (impulse) and the ego (planning).

Personality and temperament

There are some personality types and temperaments that have the tendency or predisposition for procrastination, such as maladaptive perfectionists, impulsive, avoidant, emotional, problem-dwelling, reactionary, and those with victim mentality.

The key to effectively manage procrastination is to align strategy with brain and personality systems. What tools can make a perfectionist more adaptive? An impulsive/avoidant/emotional person more task-oriented/responsible? A problem-dweller more problem-solver? A reactionary more visionary? What will it take for a person with victim mentality to adapt a creator mindset?

Incentives

Chronic procrastination happens when a person who is always procrastinating starts to attach the sense of relief and accomplishment to the act of delaying instead of the actual doing. This is when it becomes a way of thinking and living.

The person may also get incentives for procrastination such as being able to work best under pressure, an all-nighter resulting to an A+ in school, beating the deadline, getting good results despite of procrastination, being perceived as cool by colleagues, and not being perceived as workaholic.

Most of the time, there is also lack of external incentive for doing things on time or ahead of time.

Genes and environment

Procrastination is partly hereditary and evolutionary. Our ancestors benefitted from living in the present and acting impulsively to survive their environment in the wild. But before you go blaming your parents and ancestors, you have to know that it's 50-50: 50% due to genetic influences, 50% due to environmental influences.

The urge to procrastinate is in our DNA and all around us.

Maybe you saw how your parents procrastinate in some aspects of their lives such as putting off household chores or not spending enough time with you.

Then maybe you read about people procrastinating in your social media feed, and it validates your own procrastination. Perhaps you equate slacking off to being in the moment. Maybe you use "you only live once" mentality to engage in leisure activities rather than setting and accomplishing your personal goals.

Amid all these influences, at the end of the day, it's 100% personal choice. It's how you react to all these internal and external factors.

The predisposition in your blood and the environment sometimes support dilly-dallying. But you are not just your blood cells and your surroundings. You have a brain for thinking, a heart for pumping your blood, and a body for acting out.

You cannot change your parents, least of all your ancestors who are dead anyway. You cannot change other people who post their lives and choices on social media. Others may argue that you cannot totally change your personality and temperament.

But you can change your interpretation and action. You can change your mindset, and you can create habits that can minimize procrastination.

For others, choosing to act can be quite simple. They just need gentle nudges such as positive motivation, step-by-step guide, or reminders that can trigger behavior.

For others, especially those who procrastinate habitually, they may feel that it is not as simple. It may require major change in their mindset and attitude.

The next chapters will provide tools and options on how you can deal with procrastination, whether you are an occasional, situational, or perennial procrastinator.

Chapter 4: Signs And Examples Of Procrastination

Listed below are a few different examples of individuals who are known procrastinators, all procrastinate in a relatively similar manner, but each has different circumstances.

Julie is a full-time student who works full-time at an office job. Her mornings consist of her jumping out of bed thirty minutes before she needs to leave, showering, brushing her teeth, throwing on her clothes and rushing out the door. She grabs breakfast on the way, going through a drive through. She makes coffee at work, even though she hates the coffee at work – she just doesn't have time in the morning to make it at her house, so she says.

She rushes into work, sets her things down and makes a cup of coffee. She shuffles items around on her desk to get herself situated and sets her coffee beside her. She continues working, getting emails from clients, looking around at the sticky notes that decorate her cubicle, trying to see if she has contacted anyone she needed to contact and completed other various tasks that are scribbled on the neon sticky notes. By the time lunch rolls around, she has a headache from stress. She eats a yogurt for lunch and grabs a can of soda from the vending machine before heading back to her desk.

At the end of the day, she grabs her things and bolts out the door to the car and heads to school. She has an hour before class to get her homework done, so she sits on her laptop in the school library completing as much as possible. Julie is not a straight "A" student because she says she has no time to be. Instead, Julie gets "B's" on almost all of her work, passing major exams with average scores. She makes the joke "C's get degrees!"

even though she hates herself for not trying harder, she just feels so exhausted.

She heads to class, takes notes and turns in her homework, leaves class and heads home. Once home, she sets everything down and heads to the couch, sitting down with a snack and watching television. She has homework to do but feels as though she would "go insane" if she didn't get some mind numbing action in for the day. She ends up watching television for 3 hours before making dinner. After dinner, she goes back to the living room and continues to watch television until it's time for bed. Debating on taking the homework into the bedroom to get a head start, she figures she will cram it in before her school tomorrow like she did today.

Going over Julie's daily routine, it is obvious there are some serious flaws in her routine that are causing her unnecessary stress. If Julie would take two out of the five hours she spent watching television to prepare her clothes and items for the following day. Pack her lunch, get the coffee ready to make, and did her homework, Julie would be able to have a completely different day. Julie could instead wake up and turn on the coffee pot, hop in the shower, grab her clothes that were laid out the night before, grab her homework that's been done and head to work with her coffee in hand. Doing her homework the night before would give her an hour after work one day to organize her desk and put a piece of paper out to make a list in the morning.

On days that she does her homework the night before, she can leave work relaxed and not rushed, and have some time to either study, read, listen to music or relax before her class starts. Her time at home will feel more productive also, instead of sitting on the couch feeling annoyed at how stressful her life is, she can get everything ready for the next day and have her homework done, exercise, and come back to relax guilt free!

Next we have the case of Frances, an English teacher who lives an active social life. Frances works every morning from 7 to 3 teaching Advanced Placement English at his local high school. Frances wakes up every morning at 5 and makes his coffee while he showers. He always has his clothes picked out for the following day, and his socks and shoes are by the door. He makes himself a bagel and sips some coffee while reading the newspaper until around 6. At 6:15 he gathers his briefcase of graded and ungraded papers and heads out the door.

Once inside his car, France's car is scattered with papers and empty, disposable coffee cups. A lot of the papers are assignments from his classes that he has graded and kept in the car for "safe keeping". Unlike the other teachers, Frances is notorious for his grading inconsistencies and losing papers that the kids write. Frances also takes a lot longer to grade papers than some of the other English teachers which is frustrating to kids and parents who would like to review how their children are doing and progressing.

Frances has met with many frustrated parents dealing with frustrated children who can't seem to understand why Frances wouldn't pass back papers that the kids wanted to keep for whatever the reason. The truth is, Frances goes out after work almost every night to meet with friends. He does not like grading papers and with Advanced Placement English, the kids are required to write a lot of papers. Five classes of 30 multiplied by 6 is a lot of papers...and Frances does not feel like he has time for that. He has talked to other teachers who dislike grading a large amount of papers as well, but it comes with the job, and it needs to be done timely.

Frances puts off grading his papers until close to the end of the first quarter of school and there are four quarters. As the end of the quarter comes closer, France's students ask about their grades and Frances is unable to give them an accurate depiction because he has not yet graded the papers. Instead of grading the papers and resolving issues with the students earlier, he waits and grades papers the weekend before the end of the quarter and plugs all the grades in. Students then come to him concerned about their grades, but he is unable to change the grades because the quarter has finalized. This upsets students who talk to their parents and then upset families begin to contact Frances. Frances gets frustrated with himself that he can't just sit down and grade papers, but he has got in the habit of coming home and going out, and he couldn't imagine doing anything else.

In order to break his bad habits and start the school year off right, Frances needs to go home every night and grade the papers from the day. If nothing else, allot Monday, Tuesday, and Wednesday for paper grading and leave Thursday and Friday as days to go out and have fun. Frances complains that his job is stressful because he gives himself so much additional stress by putting off grading his papers and not staying organized. One of the first places Frances should begin is inside his car where student's papers are scattered about. Starting a filing system of some kind will help him keep each class organized.

Among other things, Frances could save his bagel and coffee in a paper bag and take them to work with him, getting him there a bit earlier to get any extra work he needs to get done before the class begins to file in. Once Frances can get his paper grading under control by just doing it, even though he dislikes it, he will take a huge weight off of his shoulder. By putting off the things he hates, he is making himself hate it even more because he is forced to do it while under the stress of an impending deadline. People forget to keep this in mind when putting off things they hate. You are only going to make yourself hate the task even more because you are going to be forced to do it in high volumes, under a great deal of more stress than you would have otherwise. This can be said for not only teaching, but a wide variety of different careers.

Our last example is a college student by the name of Sara. Sara is a sophomore in college and is taking a full course load this semester, five classes. Sara does not work, she attends college, lives on campus and is involved in extracurricular activities. Although this is Sara's **3rd** semester in college, she still has yet to get down a proper study schedule and tends to put off doing homework until the night before it is due. Sara overwhelms herself to the point of tears when she lets her schoolwork pile up because she would rather be out with friends.

Sara often finds herself envious of the students taking the time to study between classes at the library, and of the students who take the time to actually read the chapters in the assigned books. To Sara, being in college has made everything related to school "optional," and she finds herself skipping class to hang out with friends instead of taking the extra time to study for the classes she is behind in. Sara frequently regrets not getting better grades in school and when her parents ask why she has average and below average grades, she simply states she is busy and tired.

Unfortunately, Sara's story is all too common with students entering college for the first time. Many students who come into college as freshman will be dismissed from the University or College due to academic delinquency if their grades are not up to par with the school's standards. It is imperative that students speak with teachers and older students regarding different types of study habits. Students learn all too soon that cramming information into your brain the night before an exam is not a good way to go about your preparation. Sure, you may pass the test and feel like you dodged a bullet, but wouldn't it feel better to take the test and have the confidence that you knew the answers? It is so much more satisfying to pass the test with confidence than cramming.

Instead of studying after class or before class, Sara spends time going out for drinks or food, and attending parties on campus. Whenever Sara has an assignment due, she often waits for the day or morning of to do it, adding a high amount of stress that could be avoided if she would begin work the day it was assigned. Unknown to friends, Sara suffers from anxiety and tends to want to be doing something consistently to avoid being alone in the quiet. This anxiety may or may not be related to her procrastination habits, but because Sara does not like the quiet and sitting still, studying has been a real problem for her.

Getting help or counseling on campus could help Sara solve this problem, many campuses offer counseling for students for free or for a small fee. There are also a ton of resources available for students to learn how to manage stress, anxiety, depression and homesickness while being away from home. Adjusting to a new environment can be tough on anyone but getting in the routine or habit of studying after class and figuring out what works best for you is key. One of the best habits is to form a study group with other members of your class. This ensures you are all on the same page and are able to work together to study for exams and other assignments as they are assigned.

Chapter 5: The Dangers Of Multitasking

The ability to multitask is regarded necessary skill in today's busy, modern world—and with most of us having more to do than there are hours in the day, it's easy to understand why. On the surface, multitasking seems like an opportunity to accomplish two tasks in the time it would normally take to accomplish one. As is so often the case, however, the reality of the situation is far more complicated. While the modern world considers multitasking a valued skill, it actually contributes to increased workplace stress and may be damaging your focus, productivity, and efficiency more than you realize.

As early as 2001, studies emerged on the dangers and damages of multitasking. An article published in the **Journal of Experimental Psychology: Human Perception and Performance** entitled "Executive Control of Cognitive Processes in Task Switching" showed that subjects lost time switching from one task to another compared to completing individual tasks in a linear fashion. The more complex the task, the greater the time lost—as much as 40%, the study found. More recently, a 2010 article entitled "Being of Two Minds: Switching Mindsets Exhausts Self-Regulatory Resources" showed that multitasking not only makes you less efficient at executing the tasks at hand, it also causes mental exhaustion that inhibited subjects' ability to perform follow-up tasks and negatively affected their decision making skills and short term memory. In other words, not only does multitasking decrease your workplace efficiency, it makes it harder to focus in the long-term. Studies done on high school and college students dating back as far as 1993 also demonstrated a lower retention rate among those who multitasked while studying. They performed worse on exams and were less able to recall the information they had supposedly learned even a short time after reviewing their notes.

The truth is, the human brain is not capable of multitasking, in the sense of working on two tasks simultaneously.

When you multitask, your brain is actually switching its focus from one task to another. The more familiar the task, the less your brain has to work to switch; the more complex the task, the more likely you are to lose focus and make potentially detrimental mistakes.

This may seem like dire news. The ability to juggle two tasks at once has become something of a prerequisite for most high-level employment—not to mention the multitasking involved in balancing family life with work life. Smart phones and other electronic devices mean many of us are trying to multitask almost constantly without ever realizing that we're doing it. Luckily, by making some simple changes to your daily routine you can limit the amount of task switching your brain does every day. While these changes require some discipline to initially implement, the improvement you'll see in your ability to focus makes them well worth the effort.

1: Make a schedule—and keep to it

Your mind is at its most efficient when it can work for an extended period of time on tasks involving the same mindset. One of the most mentally taxing mindsets is the decision making process—in other words, deciding what task to work on next can be one of the biggest focus breakers. Take 5-10 minutes either the night before or first thing in the morning to outline your tasks for the day, considering the complexity of the various things you have to do and the basic mindset you'll need to be in while doing them. Alternate complex tasks with more simple ones to let your brain rest between intense thinking sessions. Separating your day into sections based on the type of task makes it do less switching and lose less time.

Objective tasks that require little cognitive effort—like basic math, checking mail, or data entry—are the least complex and the easiest for your mind to switch into or between. Subjective tasks—decision making, creative problem solving, or analysis and synthesis of data—involve more areas of your brain at once and will take longer to get back into once you're interrupted. If you know there's a certain time of day you're likely to be interrupted, schedule simpler tasks during that time, reserving larger blocks of uninterrupted time for the tasks that require more discipline and energy. While some things are clearly more complex, this can also be a personal decision. If you feel more comfortable with words than with numbers, tasks involving lots of numbers will be more taxing for you; reserve the most uninterrupted time to complete these items, saving the relatively easier tasks for more hectic times of day.

It can also help to do the most complex and difficult tasks early in the day before your mind has a chance to tire, though that isn't necessarily the case for everyone. If you know your brain is more efficient in the afternoon than first thing in the morning, don't try to force yourself into an arbitrary system. Schedule complex tasks for your own brain's most efficient time for more consistent success. You may also find it harder to avoid interruptions earlier in the morning because of calls, e-mails, or the schedules of your colleagues. Even if morning is your most efficient time, frequent interruptions will negate your brain's normal high functioning during this time. If you can't eliminate the interruptions, it may be better to tailor your schedule around them.

2: Designate communication times

This was touched on above but deserves a special notice because of how damaging it can be to your long-term ability to focus. In our totally connected modern world, you are constantly at the whim of interruptions from the outside world if you don't take specific steps to prevent them. Whether it's a text message, an e-mail, or a phone call, incoming communication draws you instantly away from whatever task you're working on—and if that's a complex task, it could take up to 15 minutes just to get back into the flow, not even considering the time spent replying to the message. Silence alerts from your inbox on both your phone and computer when you're working on other things and designate 3-4 times throughout the day that are specifically reserved for communications. If you work in an office with colleagues who are prone to interrupting you, tell them when your "complex work time" is and ask them not to disturb you. If your colleagues have trouble respecting time boundaries, try putting on a Bluetooth headset; most people won't disturb you if they think you're on the phone.

3: Take daily screen breaks

Looking at various screens throughout the day can send your mind into information overload. Obviously this includes your phone and computer, but even staring at the television during your relaxation time can wear out your brain more than you may think: Commercials interrupt programs in much the same way an e-mail can interrupt your thinking time and having the TV on in the background while doing other tasks is still a form of multitasking. Even if you can't remove the interruptions during your day, scheduling yourself a couple hours of screen-free time can give your brain an opportunity to recharge. Try to avoid all screens for an hour before going to sleep, and again for the first hour in the morning. Even if you're working during this time—for example, writing out your day's schedule by hand—the limiting of tasks and interruptions will mean less work for your brain.

Chapter 6: Tips For Better Organization Of Life

When you are analyzing your already noted down schedule and you find that the it a very busy schedule or that you have very small time to do a lot of tasks then you should start cutting out tasks and things to do from that list. You should remove the least important tasks and make your day a little bit easier for you. This will help you perform your important tasks without over-burdening yourself. There are also other ways to lessen your burden, you can take help of someone in performing your less important tasks. Like you can ask a family member to go out and shop a little for you. Always keep some time for yourself, in which you only think about yourself and what things you are doing right and wrong.

Some of the problems that people face while trying to improve on their organized life are that they try to be perfectionist with everything and they wait for their mind to be in an ideal and normal state to start doing anything. This is a big

41

hindrance as if you give more time to tasks to make them perfect, you will always run out of time and would not be able to complete all your tasks on time. Same is the case if you wait for your mind to become normal for you to begin a task. You should always try to move on as soon as you think the project you were working on is complete. If you are having problem in perfecting some projects then you are best advised to take a break from them, do some other small tasks during that time and return to those projects or tasks later.

Chapter 7: Discipline Your Time

I have already mentioned putting down a list of goals and working out priorities so that the important tasks get done first, but how do you discipline your time when you are a natural procrastinator? The fact is that the process of starting a job or a task is often the hardest thing for people who tend to put off their tasks. They find excuses for not starting. They make up all kinds of reasons why they haven't started and they are usually ready with answers when asked why they have not done what they need to. Imagine the amount of mental energy that goes into excuses. It's an enormous amount of mental energy that could be used for more productive things – like actually going out guilt-free and enjoying your life.

Thus, you know that you have a set amount of work to do and we all have in life and up until now, you have successfully put off what you needed to do in favor of procrastination. Do you know what that makes you look like to others?

Ineffective

Lazy

A person with lack of responsibility

Pathetic

What you are doing isn't clever even though you may think you have the art of procrastination off to a tee. Believe me, if your life was that free of encumbrances, you wouldn't be looking in this book for solutions. Thus, it's time to discipline your time so that you are better able to put as much into life as you want it to give back. The things you need to have in your life are as follows:

Good food

Enough sleep

Sufficient exercise

You need to arrange your day to include each of these elements. The couch potato you are will cringe at the thought of exercise, but it actually generates energy. Make the job that you have to do fit into your life better by having structure to your day. If you are too lazy to walk, get yourself a dog. If you are too engrossed in the nighttime movies, switch off the TV or watch it earlier. If you don't feed yourself correctly, start chewing your food and introduce fresh fruit and vegetables and throw away the packet foods that you use as snacks. That's all they are and they are fueling your procrastination. The body can't work if you don't fuel it correctly with everything it needs. Think of the food as the fuel. Think of the exercise as the oil. Think of yourself as the vehicle. Taking care of you will go a long way toward helping you to manage your time in a way that helps you to live your life to its optimum and that means not avoiding things you should be doing.

Take a look at your list for the day. Work out how much time each task takes and then get started with the first task as soon as you have had your breakfast. It will help to set the mood, if you start your day by reading your list, getting out of bed and making it and then going on to achieve each of the tasks that you have allotted to yourself for the day, being careful not to neglect mealtimes. It also helps to put an inspirational quote at the bottom of your day's work list and this can help to get you moving and achieving.

Call to Action from this chapter

It's up to you to get over procrastination. If you do, you need to evaluate your time and make sure that you have enough time to sleep, eat well and exercise. Don't let this get in the way of looking at that list in the morning, but do make sure that you respect your body's needs. This helps to give you more energy and to feel more inclined to get things done.

If you are lazy and need to get up earlier in the morning, take a little comfort from the fact that you only have to do this for a month or so and then you will find your body clock will do it for you. Similarly, taking on a little extra exercise doesn't have to be a chore. Need to walk? Get a dog. Want to dance? Do it. All those fun activities help you to perk up your energy so that you are able to do everything you have on your to do list. If you haven't been taking sufficient time to sit down and eat your food properly, then do so because this will help your digestive system and when that happens, you feel better about life and more inclined to get up and do the things you are obligated to do.

You may not know it yet, but when you get rid of your lazy habits, you feel liberated and able to defeat any problems that happen in your life. Your attitude and your state of health will come into it, and you should learn to listen to the needs of your body and start to focus on making sure your body is ready to face the world in the best possible condition that it can be in.

Chapter 8: Obstacles That Keep You From Nurturing Healthy Habits

"An unfortunate thing about this world is that the good habits are much easier to give up than the bad ones." — W. Somerset Maugham

Even though you now know all the techniques you can use to break a bad habit and replace it with a good one, you are likely to encounter some problems that keep you from doing so.

Known as the 'barriers of breaking habits', these problems are issues that prevent you from accomplishing a certain goal. This does not mean you can never overcome them. You can battle and thwart them; however, you can only do so by gaining a deeper understanding of these barriers and by employing clever strategies to conquer them for good.

The following obstacles are the ones that keep most people from developing positive habits

1: I Don't Have Sufficient Time

This is probably the biggest excuse you are likely to give for not nurturing a good habit or conquering a negative one. Since you have a lot of responsibilities to tackle and chores to attend to, you find it difficult to take out time to build good habits or eliminate bad ones.

2: I am Inconsistent in Taking Action

Another excuse many of us make for not working on a habit is not working on it consistently. As stated before, what you do repeatedly turns into your habit. Therefore, if you will not work on a task regularly, it will not become a habit.

3: I am Extremely Lazy

Procrastination is one of the major reasons why many of us fail to achieve our goals and fulfill our commitments. You are too lazy to exercise, too lazy to cook healthy meals for yourself, and too lazy to take the stairs to your workplace, which is why you are obese.

4: I Don't Believe in Myself

As stated in the previous chapter, believing you can improve is paramount to breaking your bad habits and building good ones. If you lack self-belief and think you can never improve, that explains why you so easily succumb to your temptations and weaknesses.

5: I am Not Focused on the Bigger Picture

Most of us are in the habit of giving in to instant gratification instead of enjoying delayed gratification. Instant gratification is the instant pleasure you enjoy upon doing something. For instance, you eat candy because it makes you happy: that is instant gratification. Delayed gratification is the pleasure you enjoy later on after doing a certain act. For instance, when you lose weight after 3 months of diet and exercise, the pleasure you experience at that point is delayed gratification.

If you cannot encourage yourself to pursue delayed gratification and are not focused on the end goal, you are likely to succumb to instant gratification each time you try to break a habit. For instance, every time you think of exercising, you see your cozy bed and decide to nap instead.

These 5 excuses and issues are the major barriers and obstacles that keep you from improving yourself and nurturing positive habits. To become the kind of person you want to so you can build the kind of life you desire, it is very important that you tackle these barriers. The following chapter will address this.

Chapter 9: Asking Questions

Often people perceive asking questions to be an indication of not being intellectual enough, but that is not actually the case. It actually generates more information, answers, and solutions to improve one's productivity or ability to be effective. If you want to be successful in almost any situation, there are tips you can follow in order to construct better questions.

Think of open-ended questions — Avoid asking questions that are only answerable by "yes" or "no". Ask more insightful questions to get better answers that are more conversational.

Understand all of the assumptions in a certain task — Almost every decision made is based on what you think will be the outcome. Understand all assumptions before deciding because you might end up taking a wrong turn.

Get to know both sides of a situation — Always find out the inputs of both sides and be fair before making a decision. It will allow you to be able to find out what advantages and disadvantages of both sides are for better decision making.

Keep on asking related questions —Asking a lot of intelligent questions about a certain issue gets you to the most important part or its real importance.

Don't mind the silence — This is very common among people. They easily get uncomfortable or distracted by complete silence from both parties. Learn to use this moment to reflect on what you have just discussed and generate a new set of questions that will get you better results.

Help people find insights in every situation — An ideal approach to teach is to ask them rather than telling them something straight away what you think of the situation. Ask them what they realized and learned from the situation and you can utilize it to improve.

You should differentiate what is a fact and what is a speculation —A misconception people commit is that they mistake their own speculation over providing a fact. If someone gives you information, ask them for supporting facts or ideas on what made them say such information.

Probing questions —These types of questions also lets you find out important details which will help you solve more problems regarding the situation. You will be able to find more information related to the problem giving you more probabilities and conclusions.

Concluding questions – This will let the other party know that you have been listening to what have been saying and that you are paying close attention to every detail. This will also verify if your thoughts are correct regarding what has been discussed.

A lot of successful people ask the most important questions because it keeps them going and it makes other people feel that you are genuinely interested in engaging with them. If you are at work and you are being given ideas or tasks, ask questions to be able to get the right information you need to accomplish something. This is more effective when you want to influence people and get ultimate results.

Chapter 10: Fear Of Success- Hello Procrastination, Goodbye Success

Are you afraid of success?

Sometimes nobody can hinder your success as much as you can do. Have you ever noticed things going wrong when you are at the verge of a big success? Do you get irritated with the tiniest details? Do you start procrastinating over things that may lead you to success? Do you end up saying silly things while in an important meeting? Do you get into arguments with your friends and partners? These signify fear of success which is much more dangerous than the fear of failure. Success is quite complicated than failure although it does feel great from the surface. Attaining success implies that you are venturing into a territory that is uncharted. You are exposing yourself to demands and pressures. You would be criticized and scrutinized. An anxious part within you does not want to take the risk. Even though the thought of success can prove to be scary for you, the reality may be easier to cope than what one expects.

If you are resourceful to keep yourself balanced during the tough times, then you can manage to do so during the bad times as well. With success, you will have to learn new things and you will have to make changes. You need to be adaptive and creative for doing so. You need to remind yourself that success can

Boost your confidence

Widen your network

Shoot up your bank balance

Open up new doors with growing reputation

Cultural pressures

Economic opportunities, gender roles and cultural norms do influence everybody. These impact our success. However, these can prove to be limiting for few. These parameters can result in a conflict for many procrastinators. For instance, few people get bombarded by demands that could keep them pretty occupied all round the clock. Few people use procrastination for resisting cultural pressures. Cross cultural pressure can inhibit one's success.

Few people who have moved from their country into a competitive land feel immense pressure. They feel that in order to thrive they need to abandon their values and traditions of the native lands. While caught up between loyalty to their land and a desire to assimilate, people may utilize procrastination in order to avoid making a choice that proves to be impossible.

Common reasons for avoiding success

Success is demanding. Few people are apprehensive that success may require them to invest a lot more they can afford to offer. This is because working to attain success demands a lot of dedication, effort and time. Here are the common reasons that compel people to avoid success.

Competition

Procrastinators are under the assumption that competition that success would bring can eliminate peace from their life. They avoid successful completion of any task as they fear that they may invite competition in their lives.

Success is dangerous: Somebody always gets hurt

Few procrastinators tend to link success with the process of getting hurt. They tend to push things away as they believe that they may end up hurting the sentiments of those around them.

I don't deserve success

This is the worst of all. Procrastinators believe that they do not deserve anything when success knocks at their door. They think that they would not be able to keep up with the pressure that they would be facing after tasting success. They feel they are not worth what they would be offered.

Chapter 11: Living Room Hacks

How to Clean Your Living Room Easily

We clean our homes because it is hygienic and healthy to keep clean. Doing it systematically helps you achieve more than just hygiene. The living room is where people will spend their time when relaxing at home, and it is the first place that will meet the visitor's eye. Here are the various hacks that will help you maintain the quality of your furniture and keep the living room clean.

Rubbing alcohol for furniture fiber

For ease of application, you should use a spray bottle to apply the alcohol to stained areas of your furniture. Then use a white sponge to dab and scrub the stained area. Avoid colored sponges or cloths because they leave a dye on the couch. Allow the fabric to dry and re-fluff. Your furniture will be as good as new.

Hide Marks With Sharpie Pens

Those scratches on your wooden furniture should not make you get rid of the attractive possession, because a permanent felt tip marker would do the trick and fill up the scratches. There are wood markers that are manufactured for this purpose and you can find them in the stores or online.

If you are fixing the leg areas of furniture that is near the carpet, you will need to protect the carpet area or the floor from being colored by the pen. You do not want to deface other areas while fixing others.

Shoe Polish For Leather Surfaces

Your shoe polish can do more in your home than just shine your shoes. When leather is not well taken care of, it will get cracked and the scars will be an eyesore in your living room. Leather furniture is expensive; hence you should take care of your investment.

Simply get the right color of polish that matches the furniture and buff the leather using a clean cloth. In addition to concealing the scratches and cracks of the surface of your furniture, the polish will also shine it and make it appear more attractive. The best results will be achieved when the cloth you are using is clean and free from any polish.

Baking soda as a deodorizer

Fabric furniture can be difficult to maintain but when you follow the household hacks in this book, you will not have any trouble. If not well taken care of, the fabric of the furniture absorbs many things that make your living room smell bad.

When it gets into contact with sweat, dust and dirty liquids the living room will always be stuffy until you free the fabric from the odors. The fabric also absorbs bad smells and that is when you need baking soda the most.

It makes them fresh and clean and the room will be comfortable, as it should be. Sprinkle baking soda on the couch or sofa and leave it for at least an hour. It should cover every part of the fabric.

After that, vacuum your couch thoroughly and the result will be a fresh smelling and clean sofa!

A Squeegee Removes Every Strand of Dog Hair

Pets have to play around and even relax on your beautiful couch and, in the process, they will leave hair on the seat. It can be tiring to try to pick up the hairs with bare hands, but a squeegee will do the trick.

You may think that you can achieve the same with a vacuum clean, but some of the hairs will be left on the fabric.

A long handled squeegee will be the best because you will need to pick up the hairs on the carpet too, and bending for that duration will not be pleasant at all.

When you roll the rubber on the furniture fabric or carpet, it will loosen the hairs to form clumps, which you can easily pick or vacuum afterwards.

The Vacuum Cleaner Trick

Apart from getting rid of dirt and dust in your living room, a vacuum cleaner can be used to deodorize it. In the process of vacuuming, the machine will leave your living room with your fresh favorite fragrance.

Simply soak a piece of cotton in your favorite fragrance, for example lemon, and then put it in the vacuum bag. Start vacuuming and the machine will leave the nice smell on your furniture, carpet, floor and the whole room at large.

If you cannot do it with a vacuum cleaner, ensure that you have thoroughly cleaned the room, and then put the soaked cotton in a hidden place or corner of the room. It will release the fragrance and the air will remain fresh.

Do not Ruin Your TV; Use Dryer Sheets

Unlike the olden glass-screen TVs, TFT, LCD and LED TV screens are very sensitive and they need ample care when cleaning them. You therefore cannot use the traditional methods of cleaning, such as the use of napkins and paper towels.

Instead, use a microfiber cloth or a dryer sheet. You can soak the cloth in a little bit of water if the dust does not clear.

Do not apply too much pressure on the TV screen when cleaning it; a light, even touch will be okay. Avoid applying water on the screen directly too, always soak the cloth.

One more thing! The TV power and its accessories should not be connected to their power source when you are cleaning it.

A Basket Keeps Your Room Organized

The clutter of things in the living room will always be an eyesore, even when it is sparkling clean. Many activities are carried out in the living room, which leave things all over.

We watch TV and movies and play games; hence you will find that there are multiple remote controls, newspapers, toothpick cans and books for the kids' homework. All these are useful but when left unmanaged they will always make the living room unorganized and uncomfortable to relax in.

Get some attractive baskets and put certain things in particular baskets. It will be easy that way to find them when you need to use them, and it will keep the room attractive.

You can even add beauty to your living room by purchasing them from the art stores. Put every basket close to where the things in it are used. For instance, the remote controls and TV cleaning sheets should be near the TV. Newspapers should be near the couch where you relax and read them. You can place the basket with pens and cards near the coffee table.

This arrangement makes it easy for you to clear the living room when you need it for a particular occasion, and you will not have to struggle getting them back when all is done.

Cornstarch for a Nice Smelling Carpet

Carpet fresheners can be costly, but you can avoid the cost and get rid of the bad smells on your carpet when you sprinkle cornstarch on it. Just as you were advised to do with baking soda on the couches, vacuum the cornstarch from the carpet after half an hour and the carpet will be left smelling good and fresh.

Clear The Table After Dinner

In the morning, everyone will be put off by the view of dirty mugs and plates on the coffee table. Make it a habit to clear them immediately after use, and you will never head to bed when your tables are clattered with utensils.

Newspapers and other things that you use in the living room when relaxing in the evening should also be arranged. The baskets discussed previously are very useful in regards to this.

Put the dirty utensils in the kitchen sink and put leftovers in the trash bin, this will make it very easy for you in the morning when cleaning them up.

Dusting High or Hidden Corners

When you are through with dusting the shelves and tables, you cannot easily reach other areas with your hands or even the attachment of the vacuum cleaner. The cobwebs at the corners or high ceilings will need improvisation to clear them.

Your old t-shirt and the broomstick will do the trick. Wrap the t-shirt on the broom and you will easily clear the cobwebs and dust that settles in the hidden areas like behind the entertainment section and along the corners of the ceiling.

It is a cheap, actually cost-free solution, and you can put on the t-shirt after washing it.

Rotating The Pillows and Cushions

When all kinds of pillows and cushions are used in the same position for long, they lose their plumpness. Rotate them once in a while or every time you dust them. That way they will maintain their shape longer. Throw pillows tend to accumulate dirt faster than cushions because they are used in different ways, to rest the arms on while placed on the lap, supporting the neck when watching TV or for inclining your legs.

An outer cover that you can remove and wash will be a good idea because you can wash it easily and dry it on the line.

Clean Vomit with Baking Soda

Most of us would rather not discuss this, but at some point the need to do such a cleaning will arise, and this topic will save the day. Get rid of the excess vomit, prepare a thick mixture of water and baking soda, and spread it over the remaining patch of vomit. Give it at least a day or until it turns to powder again, when you can vacuum it until the fabric is clean again.

Vinegar and Water Removes Pet Stains

Pets are lovely to have in the house, but they come at a price. The lovely puppy will leave stains on your carpet or couch. You do not have to worry about it because a mixture of 2 cups of warm water and 2 of vinegar plus a few spoons of baking soda will clear the mess.

For a wet stain, ensure that you absorb as much of it as you can with paper towels. This will stop the pee from seeping down to the floor or into the padding of the seat. Apply the mixed cleaner on the area of the stain.

You can pour it over or use a spray bottle to soak the stained area with the cleaner. Give it about five minutes before you start blotting. Blot until it is dry, and then apply cornstarch, which you will then vacuum to remove pee odors.

Chapter 12: 11 Ways To Beat Procrastination

Procrastination strikes everybody, and once it gets ahold of you, it can be exceptionally hard to shake it off. When you envision an exceedingly lucrative individual, you likely consider somebody who concentrates efficiently at work and never surrenders to procrastination. You know, the sort who can sit on the ground in a train station with their portable PC and still figure out how to accomplish more in an hour than you would in a day at the library.

The truth is, absurdly lucrative individuals confront a similar procrastination challenges as the rest of us. The distinction is, they beat procrastination by utilising a calculated approach. To begin with, they comprehend why they procrastinate, and after that, they apply methods that overcome procrastination before it grabs hold. Anybody can take after this two-stage, research-driven procedure to defeat procrastination.

Rather than being sluggish or disordered, individuals more often than not put things off because they aren't in the correct state of mind to finish the task. Doing such places you solidly inside the procrastination fate loop. Since you've concluded that you aren't in the correct state of mind to work, you divert yourself with different errands - checking email, checking the news, cleaning your work area, chatting with a coworker, and so forth - and when you surfaced for air, you feel regretful for having squandered so much time. This exclusive worsen your temperament, and as the due date moves nearer, you feel more regrettable than you did when you initially put off the task.

Beating Procrastination

Overcoming procrastination is a fundamental matter of leaving the doom circle by taking control of your mood. With the correct procedures set up, you can steer and get yourself in the urge to complete things. The methods that follow will help you to get this going.

1. Make sense of why.

When you aren't in the mindset to work, procrastination is revealing to you something critical. It could be something basic, for example, you have to enjoy a break or find something to eat. It could likewise be something mind boggling, for instance, you're carrying the group on your back, or you're disappointed with your work. Whatever it is, rather than punishing yourself for procrastinating, pause for a minute to reflect and make sense of why you're procrastinating. This could wind up being the most successful step you take in overcoming your task.

2. Desert your deterrents.

Preceding beginning on a job, pause for a minute to deliberately consider the obstructions that may get in your way. At that point, build up a system to guarantee that they don't. For instance, you may have guidelines for a task in your email inbox, and on the off chance that you don't make a move, you'll more than once go back to your inbox to take a look at them, only to get occupied by other approaching messages. For this situation, your administration plan ought to be to get the directions out of your inbox before beginning your work. By preparing, you can keep up your concentration and stay away from procrastination. All things considered, it's substantially harder to regain focus than it is to maintain it.

3. Jump right in, regardless.

Now and again it's genuinely difficult, to begin with, something, notwithstanding when it's something that you want to do. I may gaze at a clear Word archive or remain on the shoreline on a chilly winter morning. That initial step is difficult, yet once you move - writing that initially passages or taking off on that initial wave - your mindset enhances dramatically. When you concentrate your thought on how troublesome and cruddy it is to begin, you discourage yourself from doing as such. When you make a move regardless, your mood rapidly intensifies, which helps you to remain focused.

4. Cut gaps in your project.

We frequently procrastinate because we feel scared by the measure of a project. To limit intimidation, have a go at cutting openings in it. Find littler bits of the task that you can quickly and efficiently fulfil. For instance, composing a proposal may require 10 hours of seriousness. However, you can release an introduction in 15 minutes and build up an outline of expectations in 10. Before you know it, these smaller assignments have cut serious gaps in the project, and it's at no longer intimidating.

5. Work in the normal condition.

Regardless of the possibility that you do everything else right, working in the wrong state can make you surrender to procrastination. This implies keeping yourself far from TV, gadgets, companions, and noisy spots. This isn't what works for everybody, except you have to exercise discipline by working in the condition believe it is right for you.

6. Appreciate little victories.

There's nothing very like confirming something of your schedule. To shield yourself from procrastination, you have to experience this feeling of achievement by keeping tabs on your development deliberately. Little triumphs assemble new androgen receptors in the regions of the brain in charge of reward and inspiration. The expansion in androgen receptors expands the impact of testosterone, which additionally builds certainty and energy to handle challenges. This keeps you started up and advancing. Some of the time crossing a couple of simple things off of a task is all it takes to develop the mental quality to handle something important. Keep in mind, and it's not about doing little errands to dodge enormous tasks; it's about incorporating little tasks in your day by day agenda to construct your confidence and energy.

7. Get genuine.

Defining implausible objectives for your day is an awesome approach to wind up plainly debilitated and to capitulate to the negative temperaments that fuel procrastination. Defining practical objectives keeps things positive, which keeps you in the correct inclination to work.

8. Take control of your self-talk.

Saying to yourself, "I won't stall. I'm not trying to procrastinate," for all intents and purposes guarantees that you will delay. There's an excellent review where members were educated to not think concerning a white bear. It turns out it's almost difficult to abstain from pondering something that you let yourself know not to, as your brain floats towards the thing you're attempting to maintain a strategic distance from. The trick is to move your thoughtfulness concerning something entirely different (and positive). Rather than letting yourself know not to procrastinate, consider what you will do and how extraordinary it will feel to have it done. Along these lines, your psyche focuses on the move you need to make rather than the conduct you're attempting to stay away from.

9. Try not to be a perfectionist.

Most scholars spend endless hours conceptualising characters and plot, and they even compose page after page that they know they'll never incorporate into the book. They do this since they realise that idea requires time to create. We tend to freeze up when it's a great opportunity to begin since we understand that our thoughts aren't flawless and what we deliver may not be any great. In any case, in what manner would you be able ever to create something awesome on the off chance that you don't begin and give your thoughts time to evolve? Author Jodi Picoult condenses the significance of staying away from perfectionism perfectly: "You can alter an bad page, yet you can't modify a blank page."

10. Concentrate on results.

Odds are, you hate setting off to the dentist. Relatively few individuals do. So why do you go? It result comes about. Your dental specialist is very great at making your teeth and gums more healthier and all the more charming. You likewise go because the agony of having somebody pick at your teeth for 60 minutes is no place close to the torment of getting a cavity filled, a tooth pulled, or a root canal. You go to the dental specialist since you know the procedure is justified, despite all the trouble. A similar attitude applies to a challenging task. While it might make you on anxious to begin, don't concentrate on that. Simply consider how incredible it will feel to complete things and how much more awful you'll feel on the off chance that you hold up until the latest possible time and don't give it your best effort.

11. Pardon yourself.

There's no reason for pounding yourself when you foul up and procrastinate. You may believe that rebuffing yourself will help you evade procrastination, later on, however, it certainly has the inverse impact - thrashing yourself sends you again into the procrastination doom circle.

Uniting It All

The way to beat procrastination is to comprehend that procrastination is grounded in feelings. The methodologies above will help you to turn the procrastination doom circle on its head and to accomplish greater productivity than earlier.

Work habits to boost productivity

It is improbable in today's workplace that workloads will diminish. Individuals are confronted with the same tremendous heaps of work to do day by day. Notwithstanding, if representatives can figure out how to be more efficient at work, they can vanquish their workload and discover all the more leisure time for satisfaction.

Considers demonstrating that 50% of labourers don't arrange their day by day exercises, however making schedules can help them turn out to be more productive. It is imperative to begin the habit of making a timetable consistently and staying with it to enhance productivity.

Employees ought to arrange their workload by breaking the day into one-hour increases, making a record of what they will work on inside those time frames, and posting the calendar in a visible place to help remain on track. Planning in one-hour increment makes a due date for fulfilment; notwithstanding, due dates can be balanced as required over the span of the day. There are three critical sorts of schedules:

1. Every day: A day by day schedule mirrors the hour-by-hour timetable of work which can be amended daily and guarantees that workers interpretation of tasks that they can deal with.

2. Projects: Separate records ought to be kept of every present project, alongside their due dates and needs.

3. Long term: A long-term schedule distinguishes non-dire work exercises or ventures that will be done at a later date. Occasionally, things from this rundown can be moved to the others.

Defeating Procrastination is a necessary expertise in ending up noticeably more productive, and it is the "single greatest element making individuals fall behind in their work, miss due dates, and hand over trashy efforts." Procrastinators habitually miss deadlines and tend to float through their work, bouncing from a task to another and not getting enough accomplished.

Workers that turn out to be more trained in handling offensive, schedule or demanding tasks will acquire fearlessness and abstain from time wasting. To beat procrastination, workers ought to begin their day by dealing with the most interesting assignments initially to avoid weariness.

They ought to reward themselves for achieving errands and adhering to a timetable. There are a few systems that can help representatives conquer procrastination:

* Think about a positive result to finishing a task.

* Break down a complex project into a progression of flexible steps and send them to the schedule.

* Create a motivation by promising a unique reward for taking care of business.

* Recognise that things might not need to be done privately and that occasionally an attempt is superior to avoidance.

* Delegate exhausting work that might be a vitality drainer.

Workers should likewise take out negative behaviour patterns and diversions that waste time. Sleeping late or investing excessively energy surfing the web is cases of time wasters.

To wipe out these unfortunate propensities, workers ought to distinguish their particular habits and time-wasters, and afterwards, post a rundown of those exercises that must be stayed away from. By utilising a firm, imperative voice on the published list, it will help them continually to remember those time-wasters. Workers can oversee distractions by physically shutting out interferences and closing the entryway, posting a do not disturb sign, or requesting that others be calm.

Bly proposes a few other key work habits to expand worker productivity, for example, the 80/20 rule. By and large, the rule recommends that 80 percent of labourers' achievements originated from 20 percent of their endeavours.

Accordingly, employees must make sense of what makes that 20 percent so productive and imitate it to build productivity. Different strategies incorporate building or utilising existing standard working techniques to abstain from rehashing the wheel, and changing work routines to fit greatest physical vitality levels.

To keep up pinnacle vitality amid the day, workers ought to invest the vast majority of their energy occupied with non-exhausting assignments and take consistent breaks to re-stimulate. Finally, a very much planned workspace where everything is open and copious can likewise help productivity.

Chapter 13: Habits Related To Health

Hierarchy of Needs

The psychologist Abraham Maslow, in 1943, published a widely accepted hierarchy of human needs. There were five levels of needs ranging from lowest (5) to highest (1). They were:

Self-actualization needs

Such things as sport, art, knowledge.....

Esteem needs

Prestige, Feelings of accomplishment

Belongingness and Love needs

Intimate relationships, friends

Safety needs

Security, safety

Physiological needs

Food, water, warmth, rest

All of our habits can be placed into one or other of these need categories. Those involving health, which we look at this chapter are among those ranked 5 in the hierarchy.

Inventory of your life

It was suggested that you carry out an inventory of your life in which the last instruction was to make a list of your habits. If you do not have the following habit on your list then place it there. It is extremely important and will provide a means to structure your other habits.

Habit 1: Make a daily checklist of tasks to be done

Most people who are successful have one. Presidents, Prime Ministers, CEOs and other leaders often have subordinates prepare them. The reason for this is to remove the guesswork about what should be done. The wise staff knows the needs and habits of their employers and include such things as dining, gym sessions and social meetings in with the work commitments. If possible they also leave spaces for the leaders to insert personal items.

By setting up these checklists important things that have to be done are scheduled and must be carried out. If you are preparing this checklist make sure that you have some means by which you can assign a rank of importance to the tasks so that you ensure that the really important tasks are carried out. Here are some benefits of checklists.

●They remove decision-making about what to do.

●They ensure things are done.

●Time is saved and time is precious.

What Habits Should You Have For Good Health?

The list below is probably not exhaustive but includes many things you need to consider. Some of these such as diet, exercise, and meditation are huge habits and probably need many support habits.

Eat a good diet. This was mentioned in the previous chapter and is a very large habit requiring many support habits.

Exercise regularly. Every authority on health puts great value on exercise. It should never be neglected.

Get enough sleep. Even if you have a good diet and regular exercise but get less than seven hours sleep frequently you are in danger of great harm. A shortage of sleep in the short-term causes such things as lack of alertness, bad temper, being accident-prone, having difficulty in concentrating. In the long-term, a lack of sleep can be very serious with consequences such as loss of libido and high blood pressure.

Avoid stress. Stress is something that must be controlled. Stress is the result of what is seen as threat and the body's reaction to it. Everybody sometimes has what is referred to as acute stress when a dangerous situation arises. Such stress is short-lived and good. However, there is something called chronic stress that goes on and on and can be the cause of serious health problems. There are many possible causes for this: a failing relationship, an unpleasant job you have to do, a sick family member are among obvious causes. There are ways of combatting stress such as meditation and yoga. The topic of stress is worth a book on its own.

Stop smoking. All medical authorities are against smoking. The evidence against it is overwhelming. If you are a smoker then stop as soon as you can.

Avoid too much sun. Sunshine is beneficial for us in the short-term but not to excess. Most facial wrinkling and some types of cancer are the results of too much sun.

Sex is an important part of most people's lives. Communication is vital for a satisfying sex life.

Everyone needs some fresh air. This has to be factored into a healthy lifestyle.

It is sensible to have medical checkups regularly and to be tested for medical conditions that may occur in your family.

Learn to meditate. This is possibly new to most readers and is discussed at length below.

Meditation is often associated with the Eastern religions, where meditation techniques have been used for many centuries. In the past fifty years, there has been a great increase in the use of the techniques of meditation among Western peoples, particularly for relaxation and mindfulness.

Successful meditating goes hand in hand with successful concentration, and the factors, which help concentration, are the relaxation of the body, a quiet and peaceful environment, and emotional peace. Meditation needs to become a habit.

The purpose of this meditation is to reach a more relaxed state to increase the ability to concentrate, to raise mental and physical awareness, and to attain a higher level of thinking activity and consciousness.

Chapter Summary

●Habit 1 is, 'Every day you must have a checklist.'

●Good Health Requires Many Habits, Some Of Which Are Listed Below.

●Eat A Good Diet

●Exercise

●Get Enough Sleep

●Minimize Stress

●Practice No Smoking

- See To A Need For Fresh Air
- Get Regular Medical Checkups
- Practice Meditation

Chapter 14: Start Here

Now that we've established your brain is healthy enough to fix you're ready to start fixing the problem. As with any therapy, your first task is to designate a goal. What do you want? If you successfully finish this book and put the advice into practice what do you want to achieve? This should be something tangible such as finishing all assignments on time for a month or getting to work 10 minutes early each day. Back in chapter 1 we talked about perfectionism – in a perfect world what would you achieve with a goal that was perfect should you stop procrastinating? Tip: Write your goal down. If you have more than one goal write it down multiple times. Like the ADD patients, reminding yourself of your reward can be enough to keep you on track. Consider posting these goals around your work area or in places you may need a boost to focus.

Start Small

Your ultimate goal is something you should strive for, but it's not going to be achieved instantly. Right now you should set yourself a single goal that is short term and can be achieved with few basic changes. This does not mean overhauling your lifestyle. What your small changes should not do is overwhelm your system or invoke that scary change reaction in your brain so that it releases fear and pain chemicals. If you're experiencing fear try and be conscious about it and aware – accept the fear but continue anyway rather than giving in as this is only a small task. A few examples of good small goals – endeavor to be ready on time each morning, try and make sure any homework is done that night and not on the deadline, set yourself a time each day to finish a project (around the house, x loads of laundry etc). Decide on a reward for yourself if you complete this, something that is also small and encouraging – a sugary dessert at the end of the week, a movie, a new outfit etc. Once you have decided your small goal it is your task to stick to this for one week. If you find it's too easy you can add a second task but do not overwhelm yourself. Focus consciously on the steps you need to do to make that single task a perfect success. What you are proving to yourself at this point is that you can be successful, that it isn't scary, and that you can achieve your goals.

At the end of your first successful week, you will still have some procrastination, you can't achieve everything instantly but you should have been successful in the specific task you set yourself and you should celebrate that. The reason this is important is that you have triumphed over something that was previously a procrastination. If you've always been rushed and stressed to work you know now why you were and have fixed that problem (perhaps you pressed snooze too much, chose too many outfits, took too long in the shower etc). By being successful in this first task you have unlocked what beats procrastination – Focus, Time Management, and Portioning. These three things will ultimately beat your problem because you'll be able to side step that nasty chemistry using logic over your emotions and feelings.

Prioritizing

Why did you choose that goal? Was it important financially? Was it your most common failing? You chose that goal for a reason above all others. When making decisions we use a very simple mental process that is mostly subconscious to determine how much we value the task and reward. You chose to do this task and not procrastinate about it partially because there was a determined reward. Take a look at this table:

	Important	Not Important
Urgent		
Not Urgent		

This table has 4 spaces which you can use as check boxes. Every task that you do is able to be categorized into this space, and your likelihood of procrastinating about it is similarly predictable. Think about what you have succeeded in. The task became important because of the reward, the action you previously had done on auto pilot or procrastinated about stopped being in that column and moved over. By moving it you were more likely to do it. The principal was designed by Eisenhower to help him prioritize and achieve his goals.

Here's another table:

	Do Now	Do Later
Do Now		
Do Later		X

Your tasks are now ranked by their perceived importance and how likely you are to do them. An important task will be done now, while something that is unimportant will be put off. The same applies with urgency. The field where the X is is most likely where your procrastination will take place because it's more likely that these things are a distraction and "filler" on your to-do list. By being able to rank tasks like this you'll be able to determine how likely you are to procrastinate about something and whether or not you are going to need reminding about it. Take several actions during the day which you may or may not procrastinate about, these should be things that sometimes get done but not always, which column would you put them in?

Further down we'll go more in-depth with this concept. At this point, you should be aware of whether you're putting off tasks because they're unimportant rather than doing it subconsciously. In fact, if you find yourself putting something off I want you to say it to yourself: "I am consciously choosing to put this off." And then determine why you're putting it off.

You can even quantify it with "later" or "never" if you know it's never going to get done. If something falls into the not urgent and not important box then question if it needs to be done at all or if you can delegate it to someone else. What this is doing is owning the behavior and allowing yourself to make a conscious decision rather than autopilot through.

Portioning

You could spend your entire day breaking it down into these tables but that would be redundant and time-consuming. You know what tasks are important in your life just as you know which are urgent because those are the ones you have not been procrastinating over. What we have done so far is to tackle your procrastination in small bites. By breaking your actions up into days and weeks you have stopped seeing yourself as an unproductive person, merely as someone who may have an unproductive day, which is much healthier and easier to conquer. When it comes to portioning this is the best way to handle your procrastination. Rather than stating you have a list of 30 things to do this week instead split it up into only what you have to do today, or this morning, or even in the next hour. If necessary set yourself a timer so that you increase that feeling of urgency to get things done and trick your mind into feeling that deadline rush. Much of this relies on your not multitasking. We live in a society that exists on multi-tasking which is why so many things are left half done since we just don't have time to do everything to the full extent. You need to stop multitasking. Just stop already!

Think back to the person with ADD. Even if you don't have it you'll find some similarities with their dilemma. There's so much going on that they're constantly distracted by a new task or going back to an unfinished one. How many times have you come back into a room and found a task you started but never finished then gone back to it even though you may have been in the middle of a different task. This lack of focus and attempt to do everything is why you're feeling like nothing gets completed. Each task on your list requires your full attention. Don't worry about the other tasks or those let for tomorrow, just the ones that need to be done urgently, importantly and within the time period you've set. Make sure you have your full focus on each task so that you don't get into the same trouble as those with ADD.

By not multi-tasking, you're teaching yourself to manage your time better by concentrating only on that specific time and those specific tasks. Another way you can portion tasks which can help deal with procrastination from not fully understanding how to tackle the task is to create an action plan. This is a roadmap of how you think you'll navigate the task successfully, or instructions. These aren't set in stone but having something to help guide you can make you feel less fear and allow you to get started rather than procrastinating.

The Pareto Principal

When it comes to conquering procrastination managing your time better is what makes everything work. If you managed your time well then you simply wouldn't procrastinate. In 1906 an economist, Vilfredo Pareto, came up with a formula for wealth distribution, in fact, it's very similar to what we understand today as the 2%/the other 95% principal only it was called the 80/20 rule. His statement was that 20 percent of the population owned 80 percent of the country's wealth. You're probably wondering how economics can relate to time management. Essentially it is what we have all experienced during the "group project" in school. Eighty percent of the work is done by twenty percent of the people. In project management, Pareto's Law is applied the same way in that the first 10% of the work and the last 10% (20% total) take up the most time. When it comes to your procrastination and productivity the same rule can also be applied. Start by looking at that to-do list again. We used the table before to determine whether tasks were important and urgent or not and this will work similarly but allow you to list them better. Of your list start by ranking the most important and the most urgent tasks, then work your way down to smaller and less important pieces. Once you have finished mark where the top 20% of the list is. This is your actual to do list, anything below this is an added bonus rather than something you should actually keep on the daily list and can be either scratched off, delegated, or put off until that top 20% has been completed. Part of the Pareto principal also includes risk assessment. We've already seen how risk can amp up the reward causing you to leave projects to the last minute, select items from your list that have the highest risk for causing problems and highlight those. Focus your planning on these items as they are the most likely to get done and you are more likely to be successful in those tasks.

There are limits to Pareto's law, and simply focusing on the top 20% does not make the other 80% go away, nor does it mean you can simply not do it. What this is doing is potentially eliminating the least important tasks to bring your stress level down, while giving you a clear understanding of the most important and urgent that need doing ASAP or face the consequences. To some degree you've already been doing this. You have been prioritizing the most urgent tasks because you've had to, it's simply you've made them urgent by leaving them too long and by being disorganized about the rest you're feeling overwhelmed. Having more organization to your to-do list allows you to look objectively and will stop those feelings of being overwhelmed.

Chapter 15: How Do You Prepare A To-Do List?

Preparing a to-do list is pretty much simple.

What is best now is that you do not need to have your to-do list in a piece of paper. With the emergence of technology, you can have your to-do list on your phone, computer or tablet.

I am sure you rarely leave your phone behind. So practically, your to-do list will be with you everywhere you go. You, however, need to decide on the best media that works for you.

For smartphone lovers, you can use the to-do application on your smartphone. The application is inbuilt; you do not have to struggle to look from the store. Nevertheless, you can still find other applications available from the store like pocket lists, notes, and wunderlist.

If you are not a tech-oriented person, you can always grab a pen and write the list and always refer to it when you need it.

The following steps will help you prepare an effective to-do list.

List all the activities you plan to do

List everything you plan to do during the day.

This can range from "go shopping" to "meet with the marketing team" to "attend friend's birthday." These tasks vary in nature, urgency, and the time taken to complete. In the first step, you do not have to worry about following a specific pattern. You brainstorm and list down everything that comes to your mind.

You then organize them when you feel you have listed everything.

After listing, you can now go through the list and ensure you have captured everything. Sometimes you may feel you have been overwhelmed and did not have time to complete everything. You can always seek help from colleges or family members. Do not hesitate to delegate duties; you cannot work on everything at the same time. And if you feel an activity does not fit to be on your to-do list, get rid of it.

Sort your to-do list

After listing your day's activities, you can now

sort it out.

You may start by grouping the list into a home to-do list and work to-do list or any other groupings depending on the activities on your list.

Grouping your to-do list helps you focus on certain tasks at a time depending on the importance and urgency. It is also important that you group your to-do list before embarking on the tasks.

You may not have time to go through it later, and you may end up doing activities not meant to have been done at a different time.

For you to be productive, you need to be focused on the tasks at hand. Little or no disturbance will help you be more productive

Chapter 16: Productivity At Home

Your home is supposed to be the best place for relaxation. However, it does not mean that you should not be productive even when you are at home. In fact, you will only be able to relax completely if you have been productive for a while. You need to complete certain household tasks that will keep your home clean and neat. You need to complete chores like cleaning the house, washing the dishes and cooking food.

Techniques for productivity are not only applicable at work. They are also applicable for completing chores at home. If you are efficient in completing your tasks, you will have more time to spend with your family. When you complete your tasks, you will find it easier to relax. Here are some tips that can help you be more productive at home.

41. Follow a routine

Clean your house every Monday, Wednesday and Friday. Do the Laundry every Tuesday and Thursday. Fix your bed every morning. Getting in a routine will prevent your chores from piling up. It will also ensure that things are accomplished little by little. Let your family know your routine so that they can work around your schedule too. It is important to be firm about getting your schedule followed so that all chores will be accomplished.

42. Get things done when the house is empty

When there is no one in your home, it is likely that you will be able to work faster and better. You will be able to do things a lot more efficiently when no one is bothering you. Maximize the time when your children are in school and when your partner is at work. You can even do your chores when they are sleeping. It is a good idea to wake up before everyone else and complete your tasks very early in the morning.

43. Assign chores to your children

You will be surprised by how much your children can help you in keeping your home organized. Assign them simple tasks but make them feel important even if they only contribute small things. When they participate in maintaining a clean home, it is likely that they will more easily understand the importance of cleaning up their own mess. Let your children feel like they have a role to play, and they will learn to be more participative and more active in taking care of your home.

44. Always clean up before going to sleep

You don't have to vacuum every room and organize every cabinet. Just simply put away everything that you used back in their storage areas. When you go to sleep, make sure that your house is presentable. You will be surprised how this simple habit will keep your home tidy. Ask the other people in your home to do the same and your home will be very easy to maintain.

45. Don't eat in your bedroom

This simple rule will make cleaning so much easier. You won't have to worry about ants and your bed won't be full of crumbs. You also eliminate the possibility of piling trash and eating utensils in your room. Make this a general rule in all bedrooms of your home and your cleaning routine will be so much easier.

46. Do things little by little

You will be surprised by how much you will accomplish in a day of you do little errands and tasks that can contribute to the maintenance of your home. Keeping a house clean is not a one time big time task. It is a consistent habit that needs to be included in your routine. If you do things little by little, you will not get off track and your home will not look untidy.

If there is a spillage, wipe immediately. If there is trash, throw it away. Do not say that you will clean everything all at once because there is a good chance that you will never actually get the chance to do it.

47. Look around for things to do

In a sense, this is "multitasking" but not quite. For example, when you are going up your room, check around if there is something that you can also bring upstairs. If you are talking with someone on the phone, do something with your hands.

Maybe you can wash the dishes or do the laundry as you talk away. This will save you a significant amount of time because you are hitting two birds with one stone.

48. Use life hacks

Life hacks are simple solutions to everyday problems. They are efficient and effective. More often than not, life hacks can help you make your tasks easier. You'll be surprised that you can use food for cleaning or school supplies for organizing your stuff. Life hacks will maximize the resources you have and you won't have to waste your time trying to solve petty problems. My fellow author Sarah Goldberg recently published a compendium of useful life hacks that people have enjoyed and found quite effective; you can find her book on Amazon by following this link.

49. Keep a whiteboard

Keep a whiteboard and display it in a place that you can constantly see. List down all the things that you need to accomplish. This will remind you of the tasks that you have at hand. It will also help if your family can see your goal list because they can help you with your plans if they wish.

50. Minimize time in front of the television

A television (or a computer screen, for that matter) can easily take away hours from your day. If you don't watch yourself, you might end up being a couch potato for an entire weekend. Try to give yourself a limit. Maybe an hour a day is enough. The less time you spend in front of the television, the more likely it is that you will be productive around the house.

51. Ask for help

Don't feel bad about asking for help from people who love you and your family. It does not make you less of a homemaker if you need the help of others in keeping your home clean. Ask for help occasionally, and be shameless about it. It's okay for you not to know everything, and there are a range of amazing resources available to us now. You can use the internet to learn about anything imaginable. While there are some things that you should figure out on your own, there are also some things which are made much easier by the simple task of asking.

52. Cook meals in bulk

If you are a working parent, you will be surprised by how much time you will save by cooking your meals in advance. Cook in bulk and store them properly in your fridge. You can do this on weekends so that you don't have to worry about meals as you work. I've done this myself—we try to eat a lot of fresh vegetables, so I do all the vegetable prep (peeling/slicing/etc) all in one fell swoop once per week. Think about a restaurant: they have the sous chefs all prepare the basic ingredients in bulk early in the day so they're ready for the dinner rush. If you do the same thing you can save up to 30 minutes per week of valuable time! You will also save money. If you cook your dishes all at once, you can use ingredients in a variety of ways. So in the end, you save both time and money.

53. Plan your bills and expenses in advance

Being productive involves knowing how to handle your money. If money is a problem, it is likely that you will find it difficult to concentrate on other things. You also wouldn't want to rush when you realize that payment is due. Plan your finances and make sure that you pay your bills on time to avoid any kind of inconvenience related to skipped or late payments.

54. Don't think about work when you are at home

This is applicable for the working homemakers. Try to leave your work at the workplace. Your home deserves your full attention. Don't compromise by still thinking about your work even when you have already left the confines of your office. Try not to think about work, or the tasks that have been left undone, but rather focus on the household tasks that you need to accomplish. Your home deserves as much attention as your work. Don't compromise it by ignoring your household chores and errands. If you find yourself thinking about work, consciously make the effort to refocus on your family and if this fails, take a walk, meditate, or do some sort of other physical activity to help you refocus on what's most important: your family!

55. Discuss weekly plans with your family

When you schedule everything, you know what is going to happen with all the members of your family. You will be able to prepare for any potential problems that might come your way. You will also be able to foresee any adjustments that need to be done, thus making it more convenient for everyone. Occasionally check the plans of other people that you interact with in order to discover convenient arrangements that might work for everyone. My wife and do this every week on Sunday evenings and it helps **tremendously** with making our lives sync better and it helps keep the lines of communication open.

56. Buy your groceries in bulk

You wouldn't want to find your kitchen completely empty, would you? You probably won't want to go on a lot of grocery trips either. It is best to buy things in advance and just store them properly. Going to the grocery takes a lot of time and effort. Try to schedule a once-a-month grocery trip with your family. Keep in mind that buying in bulk will get you discounts too. In the end, buying things in bulk has obvious advantages that you will surely enjoy.

57. Invest in useful household gadgets that will make your tasks easier

It is true that there are a lot of unnecessary household items in the market today. There are many things that you don't need. However, investing in the right kind of basic items will surely help you around the house. In the kitchen, for example, a sharp knife is necessary. You must also invest in cleaning tools that will help maintain your house. The right gadgets will help you significantly. If there's one thing that can help more than anything else, it's a food processor. This might sound cheesy, but a good food processor can be used in multiple ways to make dinner preparation significantly easier.

58. Get rid of clutter

Invest in big boxes that you can use as storage for clutter. Maximize the space around your home. Store your things under the bed or behind the furniture. Knowing that you have a space for clutter will significantly make cleaning easier for you. Space management is something that every homeowner should give attention to. If you plan your space well, getting rid of clutter would be much easier.

59. Take care of your health

How do you expect to take care of your home if you can't even take care of yourself? How will you be able to maintain your home if you are sick and need to stay in bed? Taking care of your own health is one of the keys to taking care of your home. Develop healthy habits and try to stay away from sickness. Exercise regularly and eat healthy in order to avoid sicknesses that will slow you down.

60. Set aside time for family relaxation

When the atmosphere in your home is light and friendly, it will be easier for everyone to be productive. Any emotional problems within your family will slow down everyone's productivity. Try to keep healthy relationships with one another if you want to avoid negative feelings. This can be best achieved by always setting time aside to bond and relax with one another.

Chapter 17: Calling Procrastination By Its Name

Admit you have a problem

We know for a fact that procrastinators have a hard time accepting their condition. While some go out their way to fabricate all kinds of "rational" excuses, others are simply oblivious to the fact that procrastination is the real reason behind their inability to complete a project on time.

As the saying goes, "Admitting you have a problem is the first step to finding a solution." You've probably heard this phrase a lot, but have you ever stopped to contemplate its meaning and implications?

In general terms, to accept means to acknowledge the existence of something or someone. It means to say YES to everything that exists around you and everything that has happened. It is a state of mindful awareness in which we look at the world (and ourselves) from an observer's perspective.

We accept ourselves, others and the world, even though we don't necessarily agree with absolutely everything that happens around us. We accept the good and the bad, the ugly and the beautiful, the pleasant and the unpleasant; we accept everything, knowing that life is made out of countless possibilities and dynamic variables that can influence our existence.

While many of us are desperately fighting to eliminate every shred of imperfection that might alter our perfectly designed future, acceptance teaches us to go with the flow. It shows us a different perspective; a perspective that allows us not only to discover the inherently flawed character of human beings but also to integrate it into everyday normality. To put it briefly, acceptance allows us to be in agreement with our authentic self (with all its qualities and defects).

But acceptance is not the same as giving up. In other words, we accept our procrastination tendencies because we want to make a change in our work habits, not because we want to perpetuate this counterproductive behavior.

The moment we begin to acknowledge the presence of procrastination in our day-to-day life is the time when we can start implementing some changes.

Acceptance enables us to act wisely and efficiently, with better results in the long run. It is the first step of a long process, which will take you from acknowledging your procrastination tendencies, to changing your work habits and finding the right kind of motivation to boost your productivity.

Are you ready to stare procrastination in the eye and acknowledge its presence?

Be mindful of your procrastination tendencies

Nowadays, the word "mindfulness" seems to be on everyone's lips. Mindfulness meditation for stress relief, mindfulness techniques for overcoming anxiety, mindfulness for everything and everyone. It seems like everywhere we look, there's always someone advocating the benefits of this increasingly popular practice. But what does it mean?

Well, mindfulness represents "a mental state achieved by focusing one's awareness on the present moment, while calmly acknowledging and accepting one's feelings, thoughts, and bodily sensations." In other words, it means to focus exclusively on the present moment, by paying attention to your current experience (thoughts, emotions, feelings, etc.).

So how useful is mindfulness in our fight against procrastination?

For starters, we cannot focus on solutions, unless we acknowledge the existence of our problem, and this is where mindfulness proves extremely useful. By setting aside our past struggles and future worries, we can shift our attention towards our current behavior.

What happens "here and now" gives us a better understanding of how procrastination creeps into our daily activities. To be more specific, we can pinpoint the exact moment when procrastination turns from thought to behavior. By being in this state of "perfect" awareness, you can drive a wedge between the beliefs that fuel your procrastination and your actions.

As you've probably figured out, the purpose here is to transform procrastination, from a seemingly "unconscious" process into a conscious, almost "palpable" act. Only then you'll be able to realize the actual consequences of your decisions and make an effort to change your attitude towards procrastination.

So how can we achieve this?

Since this strategy might seem a bit confusing and complicated at first, the best way to do it is by sketching a "portrait" of your procrastination. Immortalize each moment by using as many details as possible. For instance, you can start by mentioning the time and place. After that try to sketch an accurate description of the room, including objects, lighting, temperature, smells, etc. That will shift your attention towards the "here and now", thus allowing you to observe yourself from an outside perspective.

Now that you're done with your surroundings try to focus on yourself for a moment.

What thoughts are going through your mind right now?

What do they tell you?

Are they trying to convince you to put aside the project and do something fun?

Why are these thoughts running through your head?

Are they rational? Do they make sense? Should you trust them?

How about your emotions?

What are your feelings regarding this project?

Do you feel anxious, frustrated, tense, bored? Try to identify your current emotions as accurately as possible.

What do you plan on doing next?

Are you going to listen to your thoughts? And if you do, what will be the result?

In the end, you should have an accurate description of where you were, and how your thoughts and emotions prompted you to delay or postpone your task. Remember, you should perform this exercise whenever you feel like quitting or delaying a particular task.

If you practice this exercise long enough you'll be able to not only identify those critical moments when the tendency to procrastinate is stronger than your will, but you'll also question your thoughts and beliefs.

However, since your current goal is to simply notice the thoughts and emotions associated with your procrastination tendencies, maybe now's not the time to question your beliefs. We'll get to that later when we'll talk about breaking the vicious circle of procrastination.

Don't beat yourself up

Probably the two biggest obstacles people face in overcoming their procrastination tendencies is guilt and shame. These profoundly dysfunctional emotions are often the reason why we abandon the fight and choose to humbly surrender in the face of procrastination.

Before we discuss how guilt and shame can reinforce the vicious circle of procrastination, we need to make a clear distinction between two similar, and at the same time opposed concepts.

Acceptance and abdication, two actions that people confuse far too often. Considering that both actions mean to acknowledge and "tolerate" the presence of something (in this case, procrastination) in your life, we can understand why people don't always make a distinction between the two.

However, abdicating in the face of procrastination is not the same as accepting it. To abdicate means to give up and recognize the insurmountable character of procrastination, whereas to accept means to not let yourself be bothered by the presence of procrastination while working on a plan to overcome it.

Since guilt and shame are often the reason why we choose to abdicate in the face of procrastination, we need to get them out of the way before we can continue with our plan.

Let's start with guilt, which according to experts is very popular among procrastinators. It might not seem like it, but people who are continually postponing tasks experience intense guilt and remorse.

They blame themselves not just for their poor results, but also for not being strong enough to resist the temptation to procrastinate. It's a complex feeling that almost feels like a mixture of pain and sorrow.

But guilt has more than a few faces. It can come in the form of depression, anxiety, low self-esteem, lack of self-confidence or even a profound feeling of inadequacy.

In combination with procrastination, guilt often becomes an excuse that justifies our frequent and inexplicable delays. To put it differently, we feel guilty for putting off our task for so long, and because of this feeling, we sabotage our efforts by giving up altogether.

How can we prevent this unpleasant chain of bad decisions from ruining our productivity?

Identify the source of guilt. Do you feel guilty because you've wronged yourself or because you've hurt others?

Forgive yourself. You're a perfectly imperfect human being, so it's ok to fail from time to time.

Find ways to fix your mistake. Trying to make things right is a lot more productive than sulking in self-pity.

Learn something useful from this experience. Next time you think about procrastinating, remember what happened last time.

A mistake is neither a pleasant experience nor the end of the world. Keep a balanced perspective and avoid making mountains out of molehills.

"Shame is a soul eating emotion." - C.G. Jung

Just like guilt, shame is a dysfunctional emotion that, in the context of procrastination, appears as a result of criticism. What's interesting is that it often manifests in the absence of criticism as well. In other words, some procrastinators become ashamed of their actions just by thinking about the possibility of receiving a scolding from their boss, teacher or life partner.

It's tempting to believe that feeling ashamed will somehow make you realize the consequences of your procrastination and maybe make you do something about it. In reality, shame is just as 'paralyzing' as guilt. Even if it makes you conscious of your counterproductive behavior, that doesn't mean you won't repeat it later, when tasks become annoying, and you feel like you need a 'short break.'

First of all, shame occurs when we think about the negative consequences of our procrastination or when we're faced with the criticism that results from our lack of productivity. It is nothing more than a momentary sensation of humiliation and distress.

Second, shame doesn't cancel the obvious benefits of procrastination. To put it differently, you won't hesitate to procrastinate and enjoy the 'benefit' of not having to deal with stress and frustration, just because you felt bad the last time you postponed your duties.

Here are a few basic strategies that will help you cope with shame in a functional and practical manner:

Don't be ashamed about your shame. Feeling embarrassed about your shame is a meta-emotion (how we feel about our feelings) that often makes it difficult for us to untangle the mess inside our head. Before you can even begin to explore the origin and context of shame, you need to look it straight in the eye and acknowledge its presence in your life. In other words, you take it for what it is – a dysfunctional emotion that happens to appear in your life from time to time. No reason to be ashamed about that.

As always, recognize your triggers. In this case, it's procrastination you have to keep an eye out for. More specifically, be mindful of the feelings bubbling under the surface of your mind, right after you've decided to postpone a task or project.

Be compassionate toward yourself. Just because others might not forgive you for your mistakes, it doesn't mean you should treat yourself in the same manner. Self-compassion works miracles against shame because it allows you to unburden your soul and embrace your less pleasant side. As a daily habit, make an effort to find three nice things to say about yourself.

Silence your inner critic. Every emotion is accompanied by certain thoughts and beliefs we hold as true and insurmountable. In the case of shame, there's always that voice telling you "It's all your fault!" or "Shame on you for not doing the job you were supposed to do!" Instead of letting yourself be silenced by your inner critic, you can choose to see it as a fair warning. In other words, you take the blame, assume responsibility, and remember to avoid procrastinating in the future. There's absolutely no point in letting shame get the best of you.

The lessons you need to learn from this chapter are:

Admit your problem

Accept it as something that doesn't make you weak or 'broken'

Don't judge yourself too harshly

Chapter 18: What Is Focus, How Does It Work And What Problems Can We Have With It?

When we are focused on something, it means that we concentrate our mind and thoughts on it, that we pay all (ideally) our attention to it. Sounds not that difficult, right? Then let's have a closer look on how it works.

We can say that someone is focused on his/her work when he or she can do this work with the highest concentration and without getting distracted from it. Usually, such style of work is called hardworking and people who work like this are called industrious or "busy bees". Other people mostly have diverse meanings on such workers – some of them are jealous, because they can't or don't want to do the same, another hate them on the same reason or thinking that such people just want to impress the bosses and some people really appreciate them and want to work the same way, but they cannot understand how to do it. The truth is simple – such people can easily stay focused on different things for a long time and receive great results instead. But if you can't relate yourself to this group of people, then you are sure to have some problems with your focus and concentration.

What are the problems with focus can we have?

When you have too much things or work to do, you are constantly switching from one to another and thus, can't properly concentrate on any of them.

There are a lot of things around your working place that distract you and don't give a single opportunity to stay focused on your project or task. That can be noises, people walking back and forth in front of you, too bright or too dim light, it can be cold in the office or too hot, you can have an uncomfortable chair and so on.

You procrastinate a lot. If you have a to-do list, but you always put something off, like paying bills or washing a car, then you'll be thinking about it each time you remember it and the sense of guilt and dissatisfaction with yourself would distract you from solving other, more urgent tasks.

You work without breaks. You think that the more you sit trying to do your work, the more focused you become. No. You just get tired. And bored.

Social media. You may think that it is very important to always stay in touch while working on a serious project. On one hand – you are right, but on the other – you are just updating your feed and email, because "you don't want to lose something important and useful", but let's be honest – you know it distracts you from work and worsen your concentration, so stop and use social medias only on brakes.

Keeping in mind all the things you have to do. Well, that's awesome that your memory gives you such an opportunity, but keeping that amount of information in mind influence your focus on the things you are doing at the moment. Use an organizer - give your brain some rest.

So, these are the most common problems with concentration one can have. Of course, they can vary according to your individual ability to focus. Maybe all of them can distract you, maybe none, who knows. We are all different and there can't be any standards – what is usual for one, can be unreachable for another and vice versa. So stop comparing yourself to the others! You are an individual, with your own skills and possibilities. You can't get the abilities of this or that guy, but you can improve yours! And this is maybe the biggest problem with focus one can ever have – you think too much of others' abilities, comparing yourself to the others instead of working hard on what you have and trying to improve it. Concentrate on your own skills, focus on YOUR FOCUS and you'll reach the great result.

Chapter 19: Turningprocrastination Into Productivity

There is no denying that some of us could really fall so deep into procrastination that no piece of advice could get us out of there. So, what should you do when this is the case? Will you allow your life to get ruined? Of course, things should not go to this scenario! In movies, it is a common story twist to have the "nuclear option" when all else has failed. This is also true when it comes to the challenge of beating deeply rooted procrastination.

Among psychologists and life coaches, there is this strategy called "**structured procrastination**". Taking the technical theme of these words, it simply means turning procrastination into productivity. For this chapter, you will have to cast off previous knowledge of fancy tips and ideas about turning procrastination into something better. We are not saying that the strategy mentioned above is the best but one thing is proven about it: it really works.

So, how does this strategy work? The ever famous to-do list is needed here. Now, mark your task as the "most important" item in the list. This is that task that you've been dreading to do and which you have finally decided to put on hold. Now, look at the current list that you have and add in those tasks or chores that you need to do for the day. These could be arranged according to urgency or any parameter that you like. By this time, the list should have grown longer and more detailed. Things like "washing the dishes" or "downloading the latest episode of **NCIS**" should have been included in that list.

The next step is to rank the items in the list in a manner that those with more flexible deadlines are put in the "priority" category. This will definitely put the task you've been holding off on the lower part of the list. Take note that since this once important task has been demoted down the list, it becomes more attractive for your unconscious mind to work on it.

Go ahead and do your dishes on the sink. While doing this, take a look at the list once more. You'll be tempted to procrastinate on washing the dishes and shift to doing the "important task" that has been moved down the list. This is procrastination being put to work!

John Perry, emeritus professor of philosophy at Stanford University, reminded people that the power of this technique depends on their ability for self-deception. True enough, if you will look at it, you are just tricking yourself into working towards those tasks that have distorted priority levels. Of course, this should not worry you. Many studies have revealed that those who procrastinate habitually are not really that good in self-deception. It is their minds that go to work when it comes to mixing up the concept of short and long-term priorities.

Is there more to this strategy? Of course there is! Remember the guilt that comes with your inability to finish off tasks? Take a look at it now as it has transformed into motivation during the process of structured procrastination! When you see things on that list getting done one after another, this is when you will realize that you have turned procrastination into productivity. Yes, there are still many tips that other information sources can enumerate when it comes to beating procrastination. However, there is no doubt that this strategy is the simplest yet most effective!

Chapter 20: When Procrastination Helps You To Get Things Done

Procrastinators shouldn't all be put under one umbrella. They get a bad reputation for lacking discipline or being lazy, but some people have mastered a way of procrastinating in a way that works for them. Often that means that when they're avoiding a certain task, they make sure to do instead of something that is also constructive but suits them more at that particular moment in time.

Why it Sometimes Works

Many psychologists believe that procrastination is a side effect of being a perfectionist. The reason is that perfectionists tend to either have high standards for themselves or fear not being able to complete the job in the best way possible. Take the example of a parent planning a birthday party for their child. They want everything to be perfect, so they research cake designs, party favors and games months ahead of time. But they can't decide because nothing looks quite perfect. As a result, they're left scrambling for a cake at the last minute and end up settling for something they would never have considered settling for when they first started researching ideas.

A similar way of thinking is that by procrastinating, you're permitting yourself not to do an amazing job because perhaps a perfect job wasn't required in the first place. Perfection was only a requirement set by yourself, not by others. And without solid guidelines, one person's idea of perfection is going to be different from another's.

If you're trying to look at the bright side of procrastination, check out this list of benefits that some procrastinators swear by:

Procrastination could make you more efficient. Think of it this way, if you're given a task that is due in one week, and start it right away, you know that you have plenty of time to do it right. So you might do it more slowly than if you procrastinated. Procrastination can force a sense of urgency that encourages you to focus only on that one task, and finish it in less time. Keep in mind. However, you may be sacrificing quality.

You may work best under pressure. Not everyone works well under pressure, but depending on the task at hand, there may be nothing wrong with procrastinating, as long as you finish it by the desired expectations.

You could reduce unnecessary efforts. Imagine starting something as soon as it is asked of you and then being told that your efforts are no longer needed. You wasted time and energy getting it over with while you could have been doing something else.

There's an adrenaline rush that comes with finally finishing a task. It feels amazing when you finally finish something that's been at the back of your mind over an extended period. That adrenaline rush can be addicting.

There's something called "active procrastination" that can help you get more things done. If you're an active procrastinator, you are probably cleaning up everything on your to-do list except that one big thing that you don't want to do. That can be a good thing, of course, as long as you tackle that looming task sooner than later.

Somehow, tasks magically disappear. Although this is written tongue-in-cheek, it is common to feel super motivated when we take the initiative to write out our to-do lists. Although that is a fantastic first step to take in beating procrastination, we often write things on that list that maybe hold little value and lack any consequence for not doing them. For example, "Clean out my desk drawers," may be on your list. But does that even affect anyone but you? By the time you revisit that list, you may wonder why you put it on there, to begin with. Maybe you've cleaned it out by then anyway. The point is, the little tasks have a way of weaning themselves off your to-do list when you procrastinate because you realize they probably shouldn't have been on the list anyway.

Procrastination has a strange way of highlighting the things that matter most to you. Think about it, you're not likely to put off the things you enjoy doing, are you? Well, at least not if you're a procrastinator. The people who don't tend to procrastinate may have the discipline to tell themselves, "I won't let myself go have fun until I complete the task I promised myself I'd do." But for procrastinators, that task can wait until the fun is over.

If you're struggling to get something done, then ask yourself why it's on your to-do list, to begin with. If the answer is obvious, stick with it. But if you can't answer that question, maybe it isn't important enough of a task at all, and maybe you should be focusing your attention on other things.

Procrastination brings out your creativity. When you hide that task in the deep crevices of your brain, you may not be ready to conquer it, but it is still sitting there at the back of your mind. While it sits collecting dust, you may think of ways to make the result even better. In other words, procrastinating may allow you to be more thoughtful of a task than you would have been if you'd tackled it sooner.

Procrastination may help you in the decision-making process. Although the inability to make a decision can be a double-edged sword and can contribute to procrastination, there are times when waiting before you decide can be beneficial. Being impulsive and making a decision just to get it out of the way isn't always smart. But by taking the time to consider all of your options, as long as your delay doesn't affect anyone negatively, can show that you took all factors into account and were thoughtful about the process.

How to Benefit from Procrastination

The key to making the best of your tendency to procrastinate is that when you don't feel like doing a particular task, you substitute it for something else that needs to get done. Take a writer, for example. They may not have the creative energy to sit down and write a book at a given time, but they may have smaller, more manageable projects that they can focus on instead. Getting those smaller projects out of the way helps clear the way for the bigger ones, both by clearing the mind of distractions and by allowing themselves a bigger chunk of time to work on it.

Although procrastinating isn't recommended, and you really should try to put an end to the habit for good, it won't happen overnight. If you're taking baby steps, and know that it isn't realistic for you to stop procrastinating with the snap of a finger, consider the following tips for making the most out of your procrastination habits and reaping the benefits:

Make use of the adrenaline rush that accompanies a fast-approaching deadline. That sudden fear of, "Oh no. I need to finish that task now," creates a sense of urgency that can wake us up. The rush of adrenaline can help us work faster and help us stay laser-focused, so we get the job done.

Don't be afraid to ask for help. If you're struggling to get things done, then ask for help. Is there anything you can delegate to another team member or even another family member? It isn't uncommon for parents, especially mothers, to feel like they're the only ones who can get things done the way they want them done. But that mindset is one that can be exhausting. There is nothing wrong with taking a look at your list and asking someone else to pick up the slack once in a while.

Prioritize constantly. This skill is mentioned all over this book, but it is worth being repeated. You probably have plenty of things in the way of accomplishing what's important. It is important to know which tasks can be pushed aside and which ones are high priorities. Put the most important tasks with the most urgent deadlines at the very top of your list.

You should also consider the value of each task by first weighing their importance. Allocate more time toward tasks that are most important and hold the most value. Allocate less time to those that are less important and that aren't of significant value. The more important tasks are usually the ones that affect other people somehow.

Keeping a calendar or a to-do list helps. Have a short-term one (daily) and a long-term one (monthly). Tackling those short-term tasks can also give you more confidence as you cross them off your list, and motivate you to tackle those long-term tasks.

Allow yourself time to analyze things. Being efficient is a fantastic quality to have. But there are times when you can be too efficient. You might have a big project with a lot of moving parts and deadlines. When all of those moving parts are relying on you to make a decision, you obviously want to make that decision quickly to get the project rolling and keep it on track. But making an impulsive decision, no matter how good your intentions are, could be more harmful than good, especially if new information comes into play that you could have used to influence your decision if you would have waited a little longer.

Use the habit of procrastination to create a better balance between your work life and your personal life. Although it can be counterintuitive to procrastinate for the sake of improving your work-life balance, there is one benefit. You might start to realize what's most important to you, as long as you realize you're procrastinating and take steps to put things into perspective. For example, if you put off a task to spend your child's birthday with him or exercise for a half hour or do anything that helps better you as a person, go for it! The key is to find balance and to allocate an appropriate amount of time to your goals and the things in your life that matter most.

Again, it is important to remember that everyone is different, and some of these tips won't apply to you. But if they resonate with you, why not use some of these tips to your advantage? Making the most of procrastination can be a temporary fix, at least until you're ready to commit to the process of completely tackling procrastination for good.

Chapter 21: Increase Your Mental Toughness

Mental toughness will definitely help you become more self-disciplined and reach your goals. Instead of being prone to procrastination and leaving tasks for the last minute, you will be able to come up with your to-do list and work through your list. Things such as frustration, discomfort, a lack of self-control and instant gratification will not affect you as much because you will have the willpower to resist them.

Buta mental toughness is not born in a day.

You have to work for it. You have to train your mind to resist temptation and focus on accomplishing your tasks. Think of your mind as you would a muscle. The more you train it, the better it will serve you. If you enhance your mental toughness, you will greatly increase your chances of success in life. There are various ways you can increase mental toughness. Below are some of them:

Practice Meditation

Meditation is a great way to improve your mental toughness. It forces you to relax and look inwards. It gives your brain enough time to sort itself out and thus leaves you thinking more clearly. It also teaches the value of living in the present moment and being still. All these benefits work to strengthen you such that you will be able to undertake whatever task you set your mind to. You can meditate in various ways:

Candle staring – Many people find it easier to meditate if they have something concrete to focus on. You can light a candle and then spend some time focusing on it. Do not think of anything else. Your job is to be an observer. This means watching silently and not asking questions about what you are seeing.

Mantra – A mantra can be a word or a phrase that you say repeatedly. When you're saying the word out loud, your mind will be forced to stick to the present. It's difficult to think of the past or future when you're busy repeating some words out loud.

Breathing – Breathing comes naturally to us. It is rare to think about it unless you smell something that catches your attention. But, you can engage in breathing meditation. This is where you deliberately focus on your breaths. Spend a few minutes breathing in and out normally but this time concentrate on that action. If your thoughts start straying, you need to refocus and concentrate on your breathing.

Visualization – Another way to improve your mental toughness is by visualizing something. Once you visualize it, you should concentrate on the picture in your mind. You can focus on the fine details or on the picture as a whole. The important thing is to spend time focusing on what you see in your mind's eye.

Walking meditation –Walking is good for you but you can get a lot from it by combining it with meditation. In order to do this, you need to concentrate on your feet and track the way they hit the ground.

Focus your thoughts on that instead of allowing your mind to wander.

As you can see from the above types of meditation, there are various ways to embrace meditation. You need to find the one that works for you. Remember, you don't have to be an expert in order to meditate. In fact, if you're not used to meditating, it would be better for you to start small. You can meditate for 5 minutes and work up to meditating for 10-15 minutes each day.

When it comes to embracing meditation, don't leave it to chance. Instead, schedule time to meditate. For example, you can decide to focus on your breathing as soon as you wake up in the morning. This will boost your mental focus, calm your thoughts and prepare you to face the rest of your day. You can also decide to spend 5 minutes practicing breathing meditation a few times during the course of your day.

Another good time to meditate is when you are waiting for the bus or traveling. You can spare five minutes to go over your breathing or focus on a spot nearby. When you are on your lunch break, you can meditate and allow the day's stresses to disappear. In other words, it does not matter where you meditate. The important thing is to clear your mind and focus on the exercise.

Let us now look at something else you can do to increase mental toughness.

Learn to Make Good Choices

The choices you make each day, can and will affect your goals. If you learn to make good choices, you will definitely benefit from those choices. But there's something you need to realize. The choices you make affect your future actions.

Think about it. If your goal is to arrival to work early, you will have to make some decisions that will lead to that outcome. For example, you can choose to go to bed early or to set up an alarm clock or to plan for the next day or to take a different route to work and so forth. These choices can help you arrive at your goal.

However, you can also decide to party the night away, or forget to set up the alarm clock, or neglect to plan for the next day or use a route that has a lot of traffic. These choices can hinder your goals.

Your goals are important. You need to make them a priority. This means taking your time to make choices that will actually help you succeed. If you embrace the habit of making good choices, you will see good results. As you look at your options, determine which option will bring you the best results. Don't just look at immediate results, but also consider future ramifications and how your choices will affect other people or other projects.

Be Persistent

You cannot give up on your quest to follow your dreams. Remember, your dreams can only turn into reality if you know your goals and take steps to make them come true. This requires persistence.

As you've already seen, habit formation takes time. This is due to the fact that habits are ingrained. If you want to create a new habit, you must work at it until it becomes ingrained. In the meantime, you may find yourself slipping back into old habits. Don't let that discourage you. Instead, take comfort in knowing that you are slowly but surely building up your mental toughness by sticking to your new routine a little bit longer.

When you practice meditation, make choices in advance and work persistently to create new habits and follow a to-do list, you will be in the best position to strengthen your self-discipline and achieve your goals. This is something you should aspire to do.

Chapter 22: Self-Caused Triggers For Procrastination

To keep you on the right track, we have also collected a list of the most common self-caused and self-developed triggers that often cause you to switch back to being lazy and procrastinating. At the end of your journey towards productivity, we are presenting you to the most common triggers you need to avoid, providing solution for how to avoid them.

Problem #1: "I will do this later"

This is a number one self-caused trigger common within procrastinators. This is basically a general conclusion: "I will do this later" that make you procrastinate, thinking everything could be done tomorrow and that tomorrow somehow never comes as you only have more and more tasks each day, making it almost impossible to achieve everything, which is a perfectly sane consequence although it is fairly negative. Then you are stuck with million things to do and you are working on all your tasks under pressure just because you thought you could postpone everything for later.

Solution: Whenever you catch yourself saying: "I will do this later" just think about all the work you will have for that later as your daily tasks will just pile up one on top of other, waiting for you when the deadline comes. Think about the pressure and stress you will be caught up with whenever you decide to postpone something for "later". All that stress and pressure is not worth it, so you will get up and stop procrastinating, focusing on what you can do today without leaving it for tomorrow. By sticking to your goals and your to-do list you are actually making sure that everything is done right on time with no pressure and no stress and no last-minute work that can be more than overwhelming in a negative way.

Problem #2: "I don't feel like doing this"

You don't feel like doing this, but let's face it: there are lots of things in life we would rather choose not to do, but we still have to, but instead of finding a way to avoid doing something it is always better and more productive to try and find the way how to do it. When you say that you don't feel like doing something, you will most likely choose not to do it, without thinking about the possible consequences. You will find million other things to do instead of focusing on the problem you need to solve, that way procrastinating for as long as you can. But what will you do when the deadline comes? That thing you didn't want to do will still be waiting with all the consequences.

Solution: As we've already said, it is always better to spend time on finding solution than avoiding the problem you have. The thing you don't feel like doing will be there waiting for you regardless of how you feel about it. Procrastinating will feel great while it lasts but afterwards you will face stress and consequences, probably not having the job well done since you will be doing it under pressure. Whenever you catch yourself saying: "I don't feel like doing this" remember that there are some things in life that we rather choose not to do, but we still have it. It is all for your sake, so think about a reward afterwards, pep talking yourself into doing what you don't feel like doing. Set up a reward after that task is done although it bores you or makes you feel uncomfortable, and use that reward as a motivation that will push you through the end of that hated task. The reward can be anything you like or enjoy. That way you will make finishing that task a lot easier than it would normally be.

Problem #3: "What if I fail?"

The fear of failing can be a lot to handle, but it is a self-inflicted psychological wound that you need to heal yourself if you want to stay productive. The fear of failure will come as a brake that will stop you from succeeding even before you even tried to succeed. By using this negative thought, repeating it in your head, you will only get further from completing your goals and the reason for that would be nothing else but your fear. Fear of failing is failure without even trying.

Solution: It is far better to try and fail then do nothing about the problem you are facing. Failure can be viewed as a positive thing if you are able to learn something from it. Even if it happens that you fail, you can learn on your own mistakes and do it right the next time. There is no room or need for fear as it will only bring you further form your goals, where you will catch yourself at the end completely unfulfilled without even trying only because you had a fear o9f failing. There is no such thing among your tasks that can't be corrected and improved, so even if you fail, you would be able to do it right the next time, which will bring you closer to success and the feeling of achievement once you complete your goals. Fear of failure, after all, can be observed more as phobia and phobias are irrational fears that keep us frozen in front of many important challenges. Don't let your fears stop you from completing your goals and being productive.

Problem #5: "I don't know how to do this"

Maybe you are stuck with a task that might be a bit above your experience or your skill set. But think about why you got that task. Did your boss give that task to you on purpose? Maybe he or she wants to test you and reward you for your progress. Maybe you got that task from your teacher as he thinks that you can do better? You are now stuck thinking how you are not able to finish the task you are given as you don't have enough knowledge or not enough experience in order to do so, but we bet there is a good reason for why you are stuck with that task. So, there is no reason not to try.

Solution: For every problem there is a solution. It might just be the case that solution you are looking for is hidden. When you are fearing that you don't know how to do something, but you still need to do it, you must motivate yourself into finding a solution. There is nothing you can't learn, especially with all the books and internet that makes the greatest base of knowledge in the world as we know it. Whatever you need to do, just take a stroll to the library and find what you need, or Google for solutions. You will most certainly find everything you need in order to be able to finish your task. That way you will, show perspective, readiness to learn new things and you will be one experience or one skill richer than you were. Self-development feels great, right?

Problem #6: "What if I thrive?"

Fear of success can be even worse than fear of failure. There are certainly some among you that feel like succeeding looks intimidating. The reason for that is thinking that once you succeed in something, you will, raise expectations that other have from you. That way they will expect more from you every other time, so failing the next time might come as worse than it would be before you succeeded. You are not sure whether you will be good enough after you succeed, so you will avoid taking any action, procrastinating as long as you can.

Solution: So, what if you succeed? Others will be proud of you and would probably expect more of you every next time and that is the thing you fear the most. Instead of thinking about others and what will happen after you succeed and if you succeed, focus on yourself and on your personal vision of your success. What will happen with your life when you succeed? It will get better and most possibly you will get new doors opened for you, striving towards other opportunities and making the best out of your talents and your new found productivity – you will be progressing. And what if it happens that you fail in something afterwards? Well, you will just learn something new, so you could succeed the next time! Whatever you do, do it for your own sake, even the things you can't avoid doing – that way you will be able to diminish your fear of success and high expectations.

Chapter 23: Putting Order In Your Day

When you arrive at work, you probably go through the same routine every day. That might mean reading your emails, answering any calls that you need to or even reporting to staff within your department on current matters concerning work.

However, one of the reasons that your work doesn't flow as well as it should is because you haven't yet learned to prioritize and take things into your stride. Part of your morning routines should include the following and these will help you to be more production and proactive and that's very importance to your happiness factor.

Prioritize

What this means doing is looking through everything that you have to do and deciding which order things get done in. You need to have four piles as follows:

Urgent and Important

Non urgent but time consuming

Banal day to day work

That which you can delegate

When you do this, you acknowledge that there are some things that others can do in a quicker space of time than you would be able to. That isn't acknowledging weakness on your part. It takes a very strong and disciplined person to confess that there are indeed things that others can do quicker than you.

Managers are made of that kind of material and you will find that if you are not afraid of delegating, then you make more friends than enemies, because you are showing trust in others. Eventually, you may even be able to sort out all these piles ready for the morning last thing at night, but for the meantime, first thing in the morning will start the habit and this habit is essential to productivity.

Next, you need to understand that your brain works at optimal levels in the morning hours, especially if you have started the day as I have suggested. Therefore, those things that are urgent need your attention and you need to switch off all of the interruptions. Even jobs that you dread doing are dealt with quicker in the mornings. Thus, switch your email to an automatic reply. Switch your phone over to voicemail and switch off the Internet and your cell phone. During the first three hours of work, you need time to yourself to get through the difficult tasks of the day.

Scientists have proven that people who try to multi task do themselves a disservice because every time that they are interrupted, what happens is that they need a while before they can get back to whatever it was that they were doing and be ready to act. Thus, let your boss know you need the morning to do the most urgent things and that you need quiet time. He will appreciate it because he will soon see the results and be very happy that he afforded you that time.

I find that if you tackle the jobs you dread first, you actually find that your mood lifts as each one of these tasks is finished with. If you need even more incentive, you can work in bursts of energy that last 45 minutes. How you do this is to determine the task that you are going to take on, and devote exactly 45 minutes to the task before you consider a break. During this 45 minutes, you devote yourself to the task at hand and nothing else. At the end of it, you can take a break to recharge your batteries, to socialize for five minutes and to get yourself a cup of coffee or a glass of water.

Then you start the next 45 minutes and do the same thing. At the end of this time, you take a five minutes break and then get back to the grindstone for 20 minutes before taking your lunch break. That way you are totally honed in on what you need to do and get it done really fast.

How do I know this? I know it because I was at one time so bogged down with work that I was heart attack material. When I introduced all of the habits and routines that I have suggested, I found I had time to spare and was able to relax more. I actually looked forward to mornings and the challenge of fitting all of that work into an allotted timeframe. It allowed me to have a full lunch break, which had been rare until that time, and it also allowed me the rest of the day to deal with menial tasks and to enjoy my afternoons, ready to greet my family in the evening without being too tired to socialize.

Once you learn to do that, you also learn to enjoy your life more and can make the work that you do a challenge. What you find when you do that is that your productivity soars and you are nicely surprised that your pay-packet also reflects the respect that your boss has for the amount of work you show yourself to be capable of handling. It's a win-win situation, because you also gain a lot of respect from other people with whom you work who will likely hold your example up as being the most productive way possible to get through the day.

Chapter 24: Developing Your Growth Mindset

The process of actually developing your growth mindset takes time, patience, and practice. This process is ongoing. You have to wake up every day and make a conscious decision to have a growth mindset and then work towards developing it every single day. The more you face it as a day-to-day experience and embrace the process, the more success you are going to have with the entire process. Be patient, love yourself, and accept anything that comes up along the way. This will ensure that you have success with your growth mindset. The following techniques and strategies will help ensure that you can successfully develop your growth mindset with very specific and intentional behavioral patterns.

Embrace   Imperfection
Perfectionism is a trait that is particularly common in those with a fixed mindset. This is also the trait that tends to hold them back from learning anything new. If you want to foster a growth mindset, you

need to be willing to acknowledge your imperfections and embrace them. Recognize that not a single person is perfect in any way. Even people who are good at things are not perfect at them because "perfect" does not truly exist. There is no such thing as being truly perfect at something.

Understand that there are going to be mistakes along the way and that you will face challenges and obstacles. Learn to view these as opportunities and lessons, and embrace your own imperfect experiences along the way. The more you can embrace this part of reality, the more you will be truly fostering the growth mindset mentality.

Reframe Your Perceptions

Many times we have a false perception that a mistake or a missed opportunity should be viewed as a "failure" or a "final ending" for something. We see them as the end of the world and think there is no possible way we could move forward or carry on towards our goals after a mistake or missed opportunity. This is a key symptom of a fixed mindset.

If you want to have a growth mindset, you need to learn to reframe your perceptions. You can do this by saying "What can I learn from this?" or "What is the lesson here?" whenever something does not go your way. Changing your perception to view setbacks and challenges as opportunities and lessons instead of failures is the best way to ensure that you always see the learning opportunities in life and that you aren't holding yourself back through self-limiting beliefs.

Learn   New   Things   Often
 Whether you think a new skill is necessary or not, practice learning new things often. No matter how large or small it is, make a conscious effort to learn something new every day. Work towards building skills and put effort towards the process every single day. Make sure that you are regularly building new skills and learning new things. This is what will develop new neural pathways in your brain, which is a

large part of what growth mindset is all about.

Avoid Seeking Approval

One reason why many people find themselves in a fixed mindset is that they are obsessed with seeking the approval of others and of themselves. This obsession results in them being afraid to look foolish, silly, or incompetent in front of anyone because this might mean that they would not be able to get approval. They also tend to frequently mistake people's reactions for disapproval when, in reality, their reaction is typically not related to approval or disapproval at all, but rather related to a single isolated event.

People who attempt to seek the approval of others often fail to take action because they are afraid of losing the approval of others, or of themselves. If you want to master growth mindset and take advantage of it in your own life, you need to break up with the idea that you are going to be able to get the approval of anyone. Approval should not matter: experiences and processes should.

Value the Process More

Those who are focused on growth mindset heavily value the process. This is where the learning, the lessons, and the life experience all come from. The process of learning is where memories are made, experiences are had, and new skills are born. Individuals who foster a growth mindset recognize this, and they are more likely to value the process over the reward. While the reward is certainly a benefit, it is rarely the primary focus of their actions or efforts. Valuing the process and investing genuine time and effort into it is where you are going to find the opportunities to increase your joy, purpose, and quality of life.

Those with a fixed mindset are often fearful of this part, but this happens to be the most important and fulfilling part of the entire process of learning anything. When you reject the need of approval and place value and importance on the process, you will likely notice a significant improvement in the amount of joy and purpose you experience in life, meaning you will have a greater quality of life overall.

Own Your Purpose

Your purpose is unlikely to be the same as anyone else's, which is why it is so important that you do not place value on the approval of others, or even the approval of yourself. When you own your purpose, and you work towards it, you are more likely to experience approval of yourself, and therefore you will have a greater sense of purpose in life overall. Therefore, the more you own your purpose, the greater it becomes. Owning your purpose is an extremely important part of fostering a growth mindset. It tends to be the driving factor behind the growth, so place importance and emphasis on this part of the entire process.

Emphasize on Your Growth

Especially when you are first transitioning from fixed mindset to growth mindset, you might find yourself putting a lot of emphasis on speed. "How fast can I do this?" might be your thought, often. This is because fixed mindset people are more focused on the rewards than the process. If you want to have a growth mindset, you need to transition your emphasis from the reward to the growth itself. Focus on the growth. Instead, ask yourself "How much can I grow from this?" and "How can I maximize my growth from this experience?" When you do this, you successfully transition to a growth mindset and place your emphasis on the growth. This will increase your ability to grow which, as you know, is the entire purpose of a growth mindset.

Reflect   Regularly
 Reflection is the best time to recognize whether you are making the progress you want to make, or if you are not growing as much as you could be. Take time to reflect so that you can see how far you have come and where your strengths and weaknesses are. This is a great time to identify any fixed mindset patterns that are still existing within' you and work towards healing them.

Abandon   the   "Ideal   Image"
 The "ideal image" of whom people are

supposed to be and what we are supposed to be like tends to be where fixed mindset and perfectionism are rooted. If you want to abandon fixed mindset and foster growth mindset, you need to be willing to abandon the ideal image and pay attention to whom you want to be and what your ideal sense of self is. Then, work towards the growth that will get you there.

Consistently Set New Goals Goals tend to be major motivators for growth mindset folks. If you are willing to embrace your goals and work towards them on a regular basis, then you can almost guarantee that you are going to learn new things. If you are not, you are not setting your goals high enough. You should be willing to set new goals and work towards them consistently. Every time you reach a goal, set a new one. Have a few on the go at any given time so that you consistently have something to work towards. If you do not know how many is enough, focus on working on one short-term goal, one mid-term goal and one long-term goal at all times. This ensures that you are regularly focusing on learning new things of all sizes.

Be   Realistic

People who are growth mindset oriented are realistic about life. They know one mistake, setback, or challenge is not going to keep them off course from the bigger picture. They know people are not going to remember one minor mistake or one minor thing that happened that may have been embarrassing or uncomfortable for them. Instead, they recognize life for what it is, they put things into perspective, and they stay realistic about their perspective. They do not let anything come in the way of their dreams or their growth because they know nothing is as big as their growth. Therefore, nothing is big enough to derail their growth.

The process of developing growth mindset takes time, and it is a constant practice. You will find that sometimes you find it easier to foster growth mindset, and other times it is harder. Typically, during those harder times is when you need to practice most as this is when the most growth is available to you. Take your time, stay focused, and practice often and you will have success in establishing your own growth mindset.

Include due dates for every task

Writing down due dates assist you in creating daily to-do lists.

If your to-do list contains a large number of activities, you might end up accidentally forgetting other tasks. As you create your to-do list, ensure you have indicated due dates on every activity as it helps you keep track of each activity.

If an activity lacks a due date, fix a realistic date that you are sure you will have the task done.

Setting goals are crucial too. If not, then you will fail to have urgent tasks completed in due time.

Also, place your to-do list somewhere that is easy to see, somewhere that you will regularly view it. It is useless to create a list if you place it in a drawer and completely forget about it.

You might think that you will stay productive or might not forget a thing from the list, but seeing a list of activities that are yet to be accomplished can motivate you into putting extra effort to complete the tasks.

Make sure to take it with you anywhere you go. You can pin it on your office board, leave a copy in your car, and even at home. A smartphone comes in handy since you take it with you virtually every place you go. Place it somewhere it will be easy to take it out and check the list of activities yet to be done. You can also share the list with someone else. It could be a colleague, a parent, a friend, or a significant other. Someone who can always check up on your list and inquire about the progress you are making.

Such people will push you into putting extra effort. It would be embarrassing to tell them you have not checked anything from your to-do list. It is a good idea to have someone to push you into accomplishing your activities but isn't it helpful to have someone holding you accountable.

Chapter 25: Do Some Quick Physical Exercises

This one is an excellent one to do for the physical types, or hybrid physical types. Sometimes, you just need to get your body moving and your blood pumping before you can get any work done. Here are a few things that you can do in your room or living room that can get your body moving and into prime position to get major work done!

1. Situps or crunches
2. Pushups
3. Jumping Jacks
4. Curls
5. Leg Lifts
6. Punches
7. Kicks
8. Squats
9. Jump Rope

These are all great exercises that you can do in five minutes. You can choose to go for longer than five minutes, but remember that the more physical exertion that you push, the more sweaty you will get, and the closer you bring yourself into the bathroom shower! The point of this is not to get your daily dose of exercise in, but to get your body moving and ready to work. You will be losing more time by bringing yourself into the shower than by doing a quick, short exercise for a few minutes.

The obvious benefit of this is that it does help you get more fit.Doing crunches everytime you get bored of your work or are looking for a distraction? Get your butt on the floor and do some crunches so that you can get those abs sooner rather than later! If people would distract themselves with wanting to do crunches instead of staring at the computer monitor at some YouTube video, then I am pretty sure that the world would be filled with a lot less overweight and unhealthy individuals! Doing quick exercises puts you one step ahead of the rest!

PRO TIP: Drink a glass of water after you do some physical exercises to hydrate yourself. This helps clean your body and also revitalizes you so that you can get your projects done even faster!

Chapter 26: Strategical Timeouts

Just like the saying goes "The person who fails to plan, plans to fail", it becomes very important for you to make sure you plan everything well especially for your work and not find yourself dreading over the deadline.

If you fail to do so, it is only going to result into stress and anxiety, which is only going to lead to more problems for you, which you want to avoid. Not only this, but also the quality of your work degrades as you try to catch up with this stress, and that is the last thing you want to happen.

Now, to fall out of this pattern and put your best forward you must have a solid plan which promises of good quality and consistent performance. You can achieve this by giving yourselves treats very now and then. Now these treats might be small or big depending upon your choice. It could even be an ice cream when you decide to finish a portion of your work and you do it.

This helps you do better and rewarding yourself of your accomplishments can help and motivate you to perform better. However, the best kind of treat which you can give yourself would be one of a vacation.

A vacation will help you to get a break from your daily routine and help you to relax and get refreshed. It will help you disconnect yourself from the same environment in which you live and rather expose you to a better, relaxing environment. It helps you to get back your peace of mind.

A vacation will help you take your mind off from your work. Stress usually leads to 'softening your brain like cheese' and its productivity is thus then compromised, and you sure don't want that. A vacation will let you take your time off so that when you get back into the game you are at your best and only presenting the best of you.

This vacation need not be long. Just a day or two will also help. You need to plan it in between your terms of work. This will help you to keep your performance quality the best. Also, at the same time it will help you to relax and not stress much while working the rest of the month. You can plan a vacation on a weekly or a monthly or a yearly basis depending upon how frequently you need to give yourself a break and how much time you need to recover yourself from all the stress that you face.

The vacation is not really supposed to burn your pocket. You can plan to go to your parents' house for the weekend. Have dinner with them, take them someplace good, spend quality time with them. Or go someplace near the city/town with your friends and family, like a farmhouse or a lake house.

The best place to relax is in nature as there is nothing that connects to you more and helps you relax faster. You can plan yourself nature trips and take yourself to the beach, where you can listen to the waves roar and see the sparkling water and feel the salty breeze over your face and hair.

Just lay in the sun and get yourself a good tan and relax, devour on great seafood. Or you can visit some place which has its own renowned culture which is something new for you to discover and you can find yourself exploring new people and new atmosphere which pretty much works like a good break for you from your everyday doings.

One of the best places you can go to is where they have a good spa and provide you with a great massage. This will help release all the tension that is accumulated in your body which is trying to contaminate your mind and helps you relax. Not only does it help you relax but soon you will find yourself dozing off and having a good night's sleep and you'll find yourself more energetic than ever.

It can be pretty much to anyplace which will help you take your mind off your work and your personal life as well and just let you have your own time and let you have your peace of mind so that you can plan better things for yourself for the days to come.

These strategic timeouts are basically breaks which you will be giving yourself that are well planned before handed while you are up on your work. As time passes by, you'll notice that these timeouts will motivate and encourage you to do better and faster work because you will be wanting to take a break and relax occasionally. This will surely keep you in good shape not only physically but mostly mentally.

Depression is taking a toll on our society these days and these are the ways how we can deal with it and overcome it. Give yourself what you think you deserve. Staying fit physically is important, but staying fit mentally is a compulsion. It really affects a lot more factors of your life, your social and personal both.

Try to invest more time in yourself there is no harm. And because you will be planning all of this in the start there is no question of you to waste time or get into any problems to not keep up with your work. This is also going to help you keep active and a lot more confident in whatever you have to present.

By taking strategic timeouts you take one step forward to improve your self. Also the productivity of your content/work will be better because you are taking time out for yourself and not compromising on quality as you will have your plan laid out while you keep yourself at your best always.

Timeouts will thus become an important factor for your consistent performance. As it will let you calm down and only bring out the best in you. You can also try out doing different things of your liking in these timeouts and plan your own adventures.

Conclusion

I hope you were able to gain a clear understanding of how to improve your focus and the different steps that you can take to achieve your full potential achieve success.

It is now up to you to take the necessary action to change your habits and improve your focus. Don't worry, for it is never too late to enjoy true intelligence and happiness because anyone can learn something new at any age. What matters is you believe in yourself.

CPSIA information can be obtained
at www.ICGtesting.com
Printed in the USA
BVHW040930220620
582039BV00016B/1111